Exploited

Disclaimer

This book is a work of non-fiction based on the life, experiences and recollections of the author. The names of people, places, dates, sequences or the detail of events have been changed to protect the privacy of others.

Exploited

A 13-year-old girl groomed and trafficked
by a child sex gang

EMMA JACKSON

EBURY
PRESS

1 3 5 7 9 10 8 6 4 2

This updated edition published 2012
First published in 2010 with the title *The End of My World* by
Ebury Press, an imprint of Ebury Publishing
A Random House Group company

The Random House Group Limited Reg. No. 954009

Addresses for companies within the Random House Group can be
found at www.randomhouse.co.uk

A CIP catalogue record for this book is available from the British Library

The Random House Group Limited supports The Forest Stewardship
Council (FSC®), the leading international forest certification
organisation. Our books carrying the FSC label are printed on FSC®
certified paper. FSC is the only forest certification scheme endorsed by
the leading environmental organisations, including Greenpeace. Our
paper procurement policy can be found at
www.randomhouse.co.uk/environment

MIX
Paper from
responsible sources
FSC
www.fsc.org
FSC® C016897

Printed and bound by CPI Group (UK) Ltd, Croydon, CR0 4YY

ISBN 9780091950460

To buy books by your favourite authors and register for offers visit
www.randomhouse.co.uk

PROLOGUE
Crash

My hands were shaking that bad, I don't know how I managed to get my clothes off. It wasn't just the shock of it all – it was the cold. I was so cold, cold to the bone. But somehow I unzipped my coat, shrugged it off and dropped it on the floor of my bedroom. The zip on my jeans was broken, the seams all split and torn, so after I kicked off my trainers I just pulled the jeans down and stumbled out of them. I looked at my bare feet, dirty and scratched and very white. Where were my socks? My new candy-striped ankle socks, I'd only got them the day before. All of a sudden I just had to know why they weren't on my feet. Then I remembered. Joanne had stuffed them into my bag. Right, then. Just the jumper and underwear to get off now.

As soon as my clothes were off, I grabbed my quilted dressing gown off the hook on the door and wrapped it tightly round me. All I could think of was a hot bath. I needed the warmth – and more than anything I needed to feel clean again. I'd run a deep bath, pour in a load of my favourite bath essence. Jasmine. That'd smell good – it'd take away that other smell, that stink. I'd soak and soak, scrub away the dirt, wash away the pain.

My whole body was shaking now, as I pushed my feet into my fluffy slippers, picked up my pyjamas off the bed and headed for the door. I was just getting hold of the handle when the thought suddenly hit me, and I stood stock still. My clothes! I could get myself as clean as could be, but what about my clothes? There was the dirt, sure, but more than that, there was the blood. What if Mum and Dad saw the state of them? What would they think? I knew what they'd think – they'd think I'd got into trouble. The way I'd been acting, they'd every right to think the worst of me. They'd think I'd got in a fight, stabbed someone, and their blood was all over me! I looked back at my clothes lying in a heap on the floor and felt a right panic. It was like the cold came back and turned me to ice. Then I felt a rush of hot blood in my head and my heart beat loud in my ears. Stay in the kitchen, I said to Mum and Dad in my mind. Stay in the kitchen. Don't come up here and see all that stuff. There'd be questions, questions…

I opened my bedroom door, quietly, and listened. I could hear bluesy music floating up from the kitchen. Mum and Dad had the radio on, and I could hear them chatting too. Oh thank God. The coast was clear.

Back in my room, I started carefully folding up my clothes, turning them inside out so that if anybody did happen to see them, the stains wouldn't be so obvious. I couldn't wash my coat, but I could wash the other clothes. I had an idea that you had to do something to blood stains to make them come out, I didn't know what. But I'd find out and put them in the washer when I could. That might be a problem, though, as Mum was very particular about the washing, she didn't like anybody else working the machine.

'You'll only go and mix whites and coloureds and it'll all run,' she'd say. 'Look what our Stevie did with his jeans when he bunged them in with sheets when I weren't looking. If I'd wanted blue sheets I would've bought blue sheets!'

I wasn't likely to do anything like that – I wasn't as daft as my brother. I'd just have to bide my time. For now, though, I'd hide the clothes. I made the bundle as small as I could, pressing down on it, and put it in the bottom drawer inside my wardrobe. I made sure to pull some other clothes, clean ones, over it. No way would you think there was anything unusual about the drawer. Mum wasn't likely to come snooping anyway. She knew I kept everything nice and tidy, she didn't have to chase after me.

'Neat as a new pin, our Emma,' she'd say. 'Just like me. A place for everything and everything in its place.'

No, the clothes were safe there. I could just leave them there, put them out of my mind for now. No reason for Mum and Dad to suspect anything. They hadn't noticed anything when I'd come in. They were in the kitchen cooking their meal after work. As I shut the front door I heard my dad say, 'That's our Emma.' And they both called out, 'Hiya, Emma.' Mum said, 'Have you had your tea, love?'

Would my voice give me away? I took a breath and said, 'I'm all right.'

'Me and your dad are just getting us tea. Sure you don't want owt?'

'I'm fine, thanks.'

'Right you are, then.' So she obviously hadn't noticed anything.

I moved to the stairs and put one hand on the banister. The other hand was still gripping the neck of my coat, making sure it was tight shut, covering everything up.

'I'm off to take a bath,' I said.

'A bath?' said Mum. 'At this time o' night?'

'Yeah,' I said. 'I were at youth club and we were running about and that. I'm all sweaty.' I lied so easily these days.

I waited at the foot of the stairs. I think some part of me was hoping they'd ask questions. 'A bath? You never take a bath at night, only in morning. Is summat up?'

But they didn't, so I'll never know what I might have said. Maybe I would have told them what happened. Then maybe things would never have got so bad. I'll never know.

You don't see it coming. You can see it in other people, you can spot what's up, something's wrong. You're a teenager, thirteen and three-quarters, there's not much you don't know. Not much gets past you. But I didn't see it coming. As I lay in my warm, comfy bed that night, just one thought played in my mind. He was my friend. Over and over – he was my friend.

1

My First World

'You take my hand, love – you'll be safe with me.'
That'd be my dad talking, his big hand
wrapped firmly round my little one as we crossed the
busy city street. I remember being bewildered by all
the crush of cars and lorries and big buses, the noise
of engines and horns hooting. Not like the roads in
our village, which could get crowded sometimes, but
nothing like this mad rush.

Safe. I knew anyway I'd be safe with my dad. I
always was, wherever we happened to be. And if
Dad wasn't there, then of course there'd be Mum. Or
Nan, or Auntie Sue...I don't think there was ever a
time, when I was a little kid, that I felt lost, or left
behind, or really worried about anything. In fact,
looking back on those early years, it was like the sun
was always shining. I know it couldn't have been,
not all the time, but that's what sticks in my mind.
The pictures are bright and clear. I feel I was always

happy, or at least contented. Life was good, and of course, being a kid, I just took it all for granted. I'd no idea that one day the light in my life would go out.

That trip to Leeds was unusual for us. We must have gone to see a film or something. We didn't leave our village very often, except at the weekends to go to a big shopping mall or to a leisure park some miles away. Mum and Dad had to go to work every day, of course, but that wasn't a long way away. As far as me and my older brother Stevie were concerned, we didn't really have to leave the village at all. So it was our whole world. It had everything in it that we needed, everything that we loved.

Some of the village was very old, but our house was brand new, in an estate called Parklands. So I suppose there must have been a park here once. There was still lots of open space, though, and all us kids made the most of it. The houses on the estate were detached, and down one side of ours there was a path, with a little wooden gate at the end of it. This gate led into the woods, and it was our favourite playground.

Nearly all the families living here had young children, so there was always someone to play with, a mix of boys and girls of different ages. At weekends and after school we'd be out there, me and Stevie and as many other kids as we could round up. The roads on the estate were very quiet, and we lived in a cul-de-sac, so we could play out safely in the street if we liked. More often, though, we'd make a beeline for the woods. We'd make our dens under trees with spreading branches, and spend hours just hanging out, chatting, making up stories, having a laugh. We'd climb the trees, and some of us would carve our initials on them. Or we'd split into two sides and play armies, hiding among the trees and jumping out to fire our spud guns at the enemy, little pellets of raw spud turned into speeding bullets. Bang, bang, you're dead! Killed by a spud!

Enemy. It makes me almost smile now to think I'd happily say that word without a care in the world. Because then it was just a word. Long before I ever knew that friends could become enemies. No, people were nice, they were nice to me, they liked me. My friends liked me, and I liked them. I wanted the games to go on for ever, but of course the mums would come out at teatime and call for us, our names echoing in the woods.

Our Stevie was usually last to come in, dragging his feet. I think he was always happier outdoors than inside. He had that much energy, sometimes the house seemed too small to hold him – and it was a perfectly good size, with two receptions and three bedrooms, all spanking new and kept spotless by our mum. In a way, Stevie reminded me of a big boisterous dog – in fact he had more energy than our spaniel, Molly. Mind you, Molly was getting on by now. She'd been Mum's dog before she married Dad, so when I knew her she was always on the quiet side, not one for going for very long walks. We'd usually just take a stroll with her round the nearby fields. She was lovely, though, the loveliest dog you could wish for. The whole family adored her, with her silky golden coat, drooping ears and big brown eyes. She was very affectionate – and that's something she shared with Stevie. He might have had his moments, his naughty ways, but he was always big-hearted, good-natured. Nothing mean about Stevie.

Mum always seemed to be saying to him, 'Look at state of you, Stevie!' I sometimes thought that he could just walk down the road to the shops and end up looking as if he really had been dragged through a hedge backwards. His hair, as fair as mine, standing on end, dirt and mud – well, we hoped it was mud – smeared all over his clothes.

I'm the complete opposite, and always have been.

I like things clean and neat, like my mum. In fact, though I enjoyed playing in the woods, I was always careful not to get my clothes or trainers dirty. And while Stevie exploded with energy, I was quieter, more contained. I think of Stevie living life in the fast lane, at a hundred miles an hour – zoom, zoom – and me just plodding along in the slow lane. And if that sounds dull for me, it wasn't. As I say, I was a contented child, and it didn't take much to make me really happy. If for some reason I couldn't go out to play, I was just as happy sitting on the floor in my bedroom with my toys and dolls round me, playing little games. Or drawing pictures – I always loved drawing, with pretty pencils, pens, crayons. Not paints, though – there was a danger I'd get my clothes mucky.

'You know, Emma,' my mum would say. 'When I were expecting you, I thought if I had another one like Stevie I don't know how I'd cope. Thank God you're the way you are!' Stevie was five when I was born, in May 1989, so Mum had had a lot of coping with him by then! She'd talk about one of his typical adventures, when she'd taken him to Morrisons, and for once she'd let him out of his pushchair. In a flash he'd disappeared, and Mum was frantic, getting on to the security people in the shop. And where was he?

Behind the cheese counter, happily eating samples of different cheeses while the assistant was laughing her head off.

Looking back, I think the difference between me and Stevie really showed up most at Christmas time. I can still see the living room now, warm from the glowing fire even early in the morning. Lots of colourful decorations hanging round the walls, Christmas cards stuck with Blu-Tack on the chimney breast, the tree sparkling and gorgeous...and me one side of the fire, Stevie the other. Round Stevie it looks like an avalanche of wrapping paper has cascaded on to the carpet, all crumpled up, the little tags torn off and flung every which way. He'd been that excited he couldn't wait to rip into his parcels and see what he'd got. But now the presents themselves are lying about, discarded, Action Men here, toy cars there, and some of them are already broken. And he's looking hungrily at me, his eyes bright and eager. I'm still unwrapping my first present, carefully winding up the pretty ribbon, unpicking the Sellotape, carefully easing off the festive paper, enjoying the anticipation of what I'm going to see. Will it be the Barbie doll I wanted?

'Emma!' His voice sounds almost strangled. 'Give us a go at yer presents!'

Well, why not, I think, if it makes him happy. So he gets stuck in and tears strips off packages and cartons while I pick up the pieces of paper and tidy them away. Good little girl!

I suppose I got used to this, people thinking I was a good girl – and not just Mum and Dad who are meant to think that anyway. I remember Mrs West, a teacher at my infants' school in the village. I liked her, and she was very helpful and encouraging to me. In fact I enjoyed school a lot, there wasn't one subject I didn't like, and though I say it myself I was quite clever, so I suppose I was a bit of a teacher's pet. Well, this Mrs West was leaving to have a baby, and one parents' evening she said to my mum: 'Mrs Jackson, if I have a little girl, I hope she's like your Emma. The nearest thing to a perfect child I've ever met!'

You can bet Mum didn't waste time telling me that. I guess any mum likes to hear her kid being praised. Looking back, I could never have been that perfect, I know that. I had my moments, got into a strop now and then. I was a kid, after all, not a little robot. Maybe I was such a contrast to the other kids, who were forever crashing about and getting mucky. Most of the time I just didn't give anybody any trouble, and grown-ups like that, my mum especially.

The thing is, if the people in my life thought I was perfect, or as perfect as a kid could be, it worked both ways. I couldn't have put it into words then, but it would have been true for me to say I had a perfect dad, a perfect mum, a – well, maybe not a perfect brother exactly, but all of them full of love and warm heart and laughs. Yes, even Stevie, who could drive you mad but could always win you round with his charm.

I think of Dad as he was then, chunky like our Stevie, always dependable. If I was ever ill as a little kid, it was always my dad I wanted. If I had a headache, he'd rub my forehead and get me a drink, make sure I was all right. And I know, because Mum told me, that when us kids were babies, Dad did more than his fair share of feeding and nappy-changing, and getting up in the middle of the night. No disrespect to my mum – she would have done the same – but there was something about Dad that was so comforting. He always had a kind word on his lips – well, unless work was making him uptight, which it sometimes did. He always took work very seriously. 'A man must work,' he'd say. 'A man should support his family.' I know for a fact that family came first with him, it was everything. You wouldn't see my dad down at the pub every night supping ale and pissing the housekeeping money away. Though he knew how to enjoy himself, all right, when he allowed himself time off. He was great company, the life and soul. He used to be a DJ, and always liked his music. But most of the time he was working.

When we first moved to Parklands – I was only two, and I don't remember anything before then – Dad's job had something to do with finance. I was never quite sure exactly what it was he did, but sometimes it meant that he sat hunched up over the dining table with a pile of papers in front of him, muttering to himself. I think he advised people what to do with their money. I learned later that he'd done all sorts of things before this job, including that stint as a DJ. He'd started in the local pit, like a lot of men round here, but he'd always wanted more out of life, so he took courses at college. What he wanted more than anything with work was his own business, and he got one. When I was about eight years old, he bought a shop in the next village, one of those convenience stores that sell practically everything – groceries, newspapers, booze, cigarettes, you name it. Now I realise he and Mum must have worked so hard to get enough money to pay for it, while they still had a mortgage on our house. He and Mum must have slaved and slaved – and saved and saved.

Mum was just as hard-working as Dad – not that it stopped her being a proper mum at home. She was always kind and loving, she protected us and encouraged us, she always looked after us and took an interest in anything we did. We always understood that while she worked most days, we were always her first priority. She worked because she wanted us all to have a good home, to lack for nothing, and I can hear her now: 'You don't get owt for nowt.' It was her pride that they earned everything for themselves, never had any hand-outs. 'If you want nice things, then you pay for them.' Well, us kids didn't pay for them – stuff just appeared. I probably thought my mum and dad just got money with a magic card they put in a machine.

We did have nice things, I remember. The house was always comfortable, there was good food on the table (Mum's always been a great cook), we had nice clothes – well, Stevie's were nice at least for a little while. Mum used to dress me in pretty little frocks and white ankle socks, and smart shoes made of real Italian leather. 'Can't beat Italian leather,' she'd say. She'd do my hair really nice, managing to get my tight blonde curls to sit right. One of the many jobs she'd turned her hand to was hairdressing – very handy for her daughter! When they bought the shop, though, she gave up everything else and concentrated on that. They worked long hours, usually from eight in the morning till nine at night. The shop stayed open every day except Christmas Day. And at first there was only the odd assistant helping out now and then.

That didn't mean me and Stevie were neglected, far from it. My perfect nan, my perfect auntie...well, they were the closest to us. Mum and Dad had always lived in the area, and most of their brothers and sisters still did too, so there were lots of uncles and aunties and cousins, a lot of to-ing and fro-ing and visiting. But it was Nan and Auntie Sue we saw most of, Dad's mum and sister. In the old days, Mum or Dad had taken me and Stevie to our infant and junior school by car, but later on, Auntie Sue took us. She had a part-time job as a secretary in an office near the big school, so that was handy. She had never married or had children, and when I grew up I realised that she probably looked on me and Stevie as sort of her own. Fine by us!

And us kids were never alone at home, at least not until I went to big school. When we were smaller, Nan would always be there to greet us. She used to have a little house in the village itself, and it took her about twenty minutes to walk to ours. Later, when

Dad bought the shop, it came with a flat above it, and Nan moved in there. She sold her house and paid rent to Dad. 'Couldn't get a better tenant!' Dad joked. Auntie Sue finished work about 3.30, and after she picked us up, she'd pick up Nan too so she could be with us all in the evening, till Mum and Dad came home. Nan would give us our tea – like Mum, she's a brilliant cook. Her roasts were out of this world, and still are. If for some reason Nan and Auntie Sue couldn't be with us, there was always another auntie to help out, Mum and Dad made sure of that. But it was Nan and Auntie Sue who were fixtures in our lives, and I loved them to bits.

After tea, we'd watch a bit of telly, then for me it was time for bed. But Mum and Dad would always come up to my room the minute they got in, to have a chat, read me a story and kiss me goodnight. They tried this with Stevie, but once he got to big school he wasn't having any of it. 'I'm not a kid!' he declared more than once.

He still played out with me in the street sometimes, and with the other kids in the woods, but he was getting a bit old for kids' stuff. He spent more time with his friends from school, and now and then they'd let me hang out with them. It didn't occur to me that they might find this little kid sister a pain in the arse.

I just knew that I wanted to be with my brother, he was with them, so I was sort of with them too. 'Any friend of yours is a friend of mine' could have been my motto. And in fact the boys were nice, and didn't tease me too much.

All in all, life ticked on nicely, with small daily pleasures, most things centred round home and school and the village itself. We did go right away from here occasionally, of course. In the summer Mum or Dad would take us on day trips to Alton Towers, or to Scunthorpe or Skegness. Every year Nan and Auntie Sue took me and Stevie to Blackpool. We stayed in a bed and breakfast place for a week and practically lived on the beach. It was heaven. And one memorable year when I was about seven, Mum and Dad took time out together and we all went to Disneyland in Florida, a real adventure. Fantastic rides, Mickey Mouse and Donald Duck, fairy-tale palaces and castles… Gobsmacking. I especially loved those rides, found them really exciting. Get me on a rollercoaster and I never want to get off. It's a funny thing, but my big, bold brother hated them. He was petrified. 'I'm gonna be sick,' he'd groan.

Still, much as I loved the adventures, I was always just as glad to get home, safe and secure in my little world.

That little world was going to get bigger, though, and there'd be storm clouds in the sky – just about the time that this so-called perfect child, this little angel, was losing her halo. Or having it taken away.

2

The Sun Goes In

'Mum, Dad – there's something wrong with Molly.'

Mum and Dad were just finishing their breakfast in the kitchen, a proper cooked breakfast that Mum always said set you up for the day. They looked round as I called out.

'What d'you mean, Emma?' said Dad. 'She were all right last night when I took her out. She's just a bit quiet this morning, that's all.'

I knew it was more than that. 'But she won't get out of her basket, and you know she always gets out of her basket to say hello in the morning, and her eyes look funny and—'

I felt a lump rising in my throat and I couldn't speak any more.

'Okay, okay,' said Mum. 'We'll go and see.'

They pushed their chairs back, and we all trooped into the front room, where Molly slept in her old basket. She was lying curled up in it, panting – but slowly, not her usual puff-puff-puff.

Mum and Dad knelt down beside her, and Dad stroked her head. 'Well, now I see you up close, you do look poorly, lass,' he murmured. 'What's up?'

Molly tried to lift her head, but it was as if she couldn't bear the weight of it. It just flopped down again. I was right about her eyes. The lovely deep brown of them was kind of faded. The whites looked – well, not white. Sludgy.

I tugged Dad's sleeve.

'What's wrong with her?' I asked.

Dad shook his head. 'I don't know, love. But she's not well, that's for sure.'

'What are we gonna do?'

Dad came to a decision. He stood up and said to Mum, 'Nicky, I'll go and open up shop, but you stay here and ring vet. Take Molly over if he says so.'

'How'll you manage?' asked Mum. I could see her eyes fixed on Molly. It was as if she was asking about the shop automatically. I guessed if she had to choose between the shop and Molly, Molly would win out every time. No contest.

'Oh, I'll give Joanie a call, don't you fret. I know it's not her day, but I'm sure she'll be happy to fill in.'

Joanie was the lady who helped out in the shop

part-time. She was always very friendly and helpful – 'Don't know what we'd do without her,' Mum and Dad used to say. She was quite old, at least fifty, but she was full of get up and go. Her husband was one of the miners who'd been laid off some years ago, and he hadn't managed to get another proper job. More money was always welcome, that I knew.

By now Stevie had joined us, looking untidy as usual even in his school uniform. He never managed to get his tie straight.

'What's up with Molly?' he asked.

'She's ill,' said Dad. 'But don't worry. Mum's gonna take care of her – take her to vet if needs be. He'll see her right.'

Stevie didn't say anything, but his face fell. His eyes were bright, and I knew the tears were close, for all he was nearly sixteen.

Then Mum was all business-like.

'Come on, you lot,' she said. 'Emma and Stevie, you get your breakfast down you – Auntie Sue'll be here in a minute. Jason, you get off now. I'll give you a ring when I know what's what.'

She stayed by Molly's side, stroking her head while the rest of us bustled about. I heard the front door slam as Dad went out, and the sound of his car starting up. I couldn't finish my cereal, and scraped the remains into the bin. I left Stevie working his way through his fry-up and went back into the front room. I wanted to be with Mum and Molly. A horrible feeling was rising in me, my stomach felt as if it had a knot in it. For as long as I could remember, the day had started with Molly greeting us, one by one as we got up. Mum and Dad always got up first, and there she'd be, long, feathery tail wagging like mad. Then it was me, and then Stevie, always the last up. We'd stroke her and tickle her under her chin, and her tail would wag madder than ever.

'It's her grub she wants!' Dad used to joke. 'Cupboard love.'

But we all knew she loved us as much as we loved her. Now all the life, all the spirit, seemed to have gone out of her. I stood gazing at her. Wake up, I said to her in my head. Get well. Bring back the old Molly.

Then there was the noise of another car.

'That'll be Auntie Sue,' said Mum, looking up, her hand still on Molly's head. 'Tell Stevie to get ready.'

I opened the front door before Auntie Sue could knock. She took one look at me and said, 'What's up?' I couldn't make my face smile.

'Molly,' I muttered.

'Oh dear,' said Auntie Sue, making her way past me to the front room.

'What's going on, Nicky?' she asked.

'Molly's poorly,' said Mum. Her voice didn't sound normal. Usually it's not exactly loud, but strong and confident. Now she sounded choked up.

Auntie Sue squatted down, and stroked Molly's back.

'Poor love,' she said.

There was just a moment where we were all quiet, then Mum stood up and said, 'Right, Emma. Crack on or you'll be late for school. Stevie!'

Me and Stevie piled into Auntie Sue's little red car. Usually we'd chat to her, get her news, but no one was saying anything today. We drove through the quiet roads on the estate, into the village itself and on to my junior school. Auntie Sue would be taking Stevie to the big school, before going on to her office.

I walked into school, hardly seeing anything. I heard people saying, 'Hiya, Emma,' but I didn't trust myself to speak.

I don't know how I got through that day. Sitting there in the classroom, I seemed to see Molly's eyes whenever I looked at a book. The words just danced up and down. 'Get a grip,' I told myself. 'You've work to do – get on with it.' So I forced the worry into the back of my mind, and tried to look as if I was concentrating. I don't think Miss Norris – she'd replaced Mrs

West a few years back – noticed my mind wasn't really on my work. At playtime and in the dinner hour I just sat by myself, counting the seconds and the minutes and the hours till I was home again and would see Molly. Some friends came up to me, but they could see something was up. All I said was, 'I'm all right, I'm all right,' and they went away again.

After school, I waited till the rush of kids was over and Auntie Sue arrived to give me a lift home. Stevie had been making his own way back now for quite a while, usually with a bunch of mates. 'Good job he gets a lift in the morning,' Mum said. 'I don't think he'd ever be on time if he didn't!'

I didn't mind waiting. I liked sitting quietly in the classroom or out in the hall, reading a book. I was in the hall today, when I heard my name.

'Emma.'

For a second I thought, Auntie Sue's early. But then I realised it was my mum standing there. Why wasn't she at work? If she wasn't at work, that meant... No, I thought. She just might have left Molly at the vet's, to get better. Maybe it wasn't worth going in to work, not with Joanie holding the fort, so she was saving Auntie Sue the bother.

When I saw her face, all stiff, I knew the truth straight away.

'Molly's bad, in't she?' I said as she joined me on the bench. I don't know how I got the words out, I was that close to choking.

Mum just nodded. I could see the tears welling up. Oh no.

'I'm so sorry, love...' she started to say. I felt as if my chest had been smashed by a hammer. I couldn't breathe.

Mum took me by the arm. 'Come on, Emma, pet. Let's go home.'

So Molly was dead. Dear old Molly, who I'd known all my life. I'd taken her on her walks, I'd talked to her about anything and everything. I'd thrown balls for her to fetch, and she'd run as fast as her old legs would take her. She'd watched over us all, wagging her tail, so good-natured she hardly ever growled. Every time we came in the house it was as if we'd been away for a long time, she made that much of a fuss of us. When me and Stevie larked about in the road outside, she'd lie down in the front garden, one ear cocked, keeping an eye on us. She was one of the family, and now she was dead.

The four of us sat together in the front room, not moving. Molly's basket was still there – you could see the shape of her in the bedding, her thick plaid blanket. Her favourite little rubber bone was on the floor beside it, showing the marks of her teeth. I couldn't believe she wouldn't come back. Someone had just taken her for a walk and she'd be back soon, coming up to each of us and wagging her tail and nuzzling us.

Stevie had burst into tears when Mum told him. His face was still tear-stained, and he was sniffing. Mum and Dad were tearful too.

Mum had explained what the vet said.

'It were a haemorrhage in her brain. A blood vessel burst. There was nothing he could do. The kindest thing was to put her to sleep, to save her suffering.'

Sleep? Young as I was, this pricked me and I felt angry. Not sleep! I wanted to shout. You wake up from sleep – this is death! You don't come back! But of course I couldn't say anything. The others accepted it, and so must I. I mustn't say anything that would upset them even more.

Now Mum was trying to find a silver lining for us kids.

'She were old, you know. Really, really old. You know a dog's year is supposed to be seven human years? Well, in human years Molly would have been well over a hundred! Think of that. We're lucky she stayed with us for so long.'

'And she didn't really suffer,' Dad chimed in. 'She went quietly, and she's at peace now.'

Well, that set Mum and Stevie off again. I didn't want to cry out loud, so I just mumbled, 'I'm off upstairs.'

'Off you go, then, love,' said Dad as I stumbled out the room.

I suppose everyone thought I was going to be in floods of tears, and wanted to be private. People knew I wasn't one for wearing my heart on my sleeve, making a fuss. The funny thing is, I didn't cry, not then. This is something I've often thought about since. At the time, I wouldn't have had a clue what was going on in my head. But maybe it accounts for the way I behaved later, when bad things were happening. And the way I behaved just made bad things worse.

I didn't have the faintest idea where it came from, but I just knew, right from the off, that I shouldn't show my feelings when I was upset. When I was happy, that was different – I could share the joke, laugh my head off, kick up my heels, join in with everyone. No covering up there. But when I was unhappy, that was different. And I was unhappy now, no question. I loved Molly. She was a lovely, affectionate dog and she'd been in my life for ever. Her going away – no, I mustn't cover it up – her death was the worst thing that had ever happened in my life. No one I knew had died before. My granddad, Dad's dad and Nan's husband, had died but that was long before I was born. So up until now, I'd never known what it was like to lose someone you loved. Up until now, I hadn't really felt pain. Oh, I'd been hurt when I fell out of a tree, or off my bike, but that was my body, I understood that. You had a bruise or a cut and it hurt, then it was bandaged up, and the pain faded and the cut and the bruise disappeared and you forgot all about it.

This pain was different. It felt as if it was in my chest, or my stomach, but I knew there was nothing wrong with my body. It was in my mind that I was hurting. So why should I want to cover it up? It wasn't as if my family went in for keeping a stiff upper lip or anything like that. Far from it. They were open-hearted. They weren't going to laugh at anyone who was hurt, or tell them to shut up and put up. Stevie was never told that big boys don't cry. He never felt the need to hold back, whatever he was feeling showed in his face and in his tears. I think the way my mum and dad looked at it was, if you've a good reason to cry, then you cry.

So why did I feel different?

When I was at school that day, I didn't want to make a fuss about being upset, draw attention to myself, so I just went quiet – even quieter than usual. Good little girls weren't loud, at least not without good reason. I'm sure some people thought I was timid, what with me being quite small and slight for my age. I didn't feel timid, I was sure I could stand up for myself if I had to. The thing is, I didn't really have to. My life was good, things went well for me nearly all the time. I could count on the fingers of one hand when I'd actually put myself forward.

Like the time I wanted rid of the stabilisers on my bike. All my friends were riding their bikes without stabilisers, and I knew I could do it too. I must have been all of six.

'Leave it to me,' said Dad. 'I'll take off them stabilisers, and help you out, hold back of bike for you.'

Great. But he only got as far as taking off the stabilisers, then the bike was stuck in the garage. After a couple of days, I said, 'Dad, you said you'd help me ride my bike—'

'Not yet, love, I'm busy. You'll just have to wait.'

And of course he really was busy, with his bits of paper and working out people's finances. Right, I thought, I'll do it myself. I marched to the garage, got the bike out and wheeled it to the top of the little hill. Then I pushed off with my foot and wheee! I rode the bike all by myself, without wobbling. That was a lesson I learned early. When you want something, don't hang around for other folks to do it, do it yourself. It was the same when I was swimming, when I was even younger, about five I think. The teacher told us to keep our armbands on, but I knew I was a good swimmer, I didn't need them. So without waiting for her to say, I just took them off and swam happily in the pool without any help.

But at the same time, I wouldn't have wanted to do anything that upset anyone. I'd bite my tongue rather than talk back at anyone. I'd rather keep the peace.

Most of all, I wouldn't ever have wanted to upset my family. If I'd burst into tears like Stevie, wouldn't that have made Mum and Dad even more unhappy, to know how upset I was? To actually see how upset I was? I wouldn't want to do that to them. I had to be strong – that's what I thought it was: strong. And strong was a good thing. Maybe that's it, or at least part of it. Later on, I would realise that hiding your feelings can give you a kind of power, protect you from someone else's power. But here and now, still grieving for Molly, I just knew I'd push that sadness to the back of my mind, keep it hidden, like the way

I'd covered it up at school. I'd know it was there, it hadn't gone away, but those feelings were safely covered up and meanwhile I could carry on as usual.

No one else would know.

3

My World Gets Bigger

I never forgot Molly, of course I didn't. I just kept her in a special part of my mind, and got on with things. At least I had something to look forward to, which helped. I was in my last term at juniors when Molly died, and after the summer holiday I'd be starting at the comprehensive. Stevie had been going there for five years and I'd heard all about it – I couldn't wait to get there. Truth to tell, I'd been getting a bit bored at juniors. I still liked going, don't get me wrong, but I knew they did things different at the comp, there was a lot more going on.

Before the end of term, our head teacher had a little talk with all us leavers. She said to me, 'You'll be fine, Emma. You've done well here, you're a credit to us.'

That pleased me – must tell Mum!

'Just one thing,' she added. 'It's more than the school work, you know. At the comp you'll be growing up, and they'll want you to make the most of yourself. And to be honest, Emma, you could put yourself forward a bit more – you're like a little mouse sometimes!'

Well, I'd heard that before, many a time. It didn't mean it was true. I'd been learning that what you were like on the outside wasn't always the same as how you felt on the inside. Still, I wasn't going to argue with the head. No matter what she said, I knew I was up for it. I was already making up pictures in my mind, wearing the new uniform, hanging out with other girls, walking to school and back again, like Stevie did with his mates. He didn't want a lift in the morning now, thought it was babyish. It was still a big effort to get him moving in the morning, though. 'I shout myself hoarse!' Mum complained.

Dad wasn't pleased at the thought of me walking.

'It's a long way, Emma,' he said. 'And you know Auntie Sue is very happy to take you.'

'Oh Dad,' I said. 'All the kids from estate walk to school.'

'What about if it's raining?'

'She'll get wet,' Mum cut in, with a laugh. Then she said, 'Our Emma's no fool, Jason. It'll do her good to walk, and she'll be with her friends.'

Dad frowned, and Mum said, 'Let her try it. See how it goes.'

Honestly, I thought, Dad must think I'm a little kid. I knew he meant well, but did he think I was still ten years old?

Dad wasn't convinced. 'But what about getting home?' he said. 'If Sue doesn't pick her up and bring her back with Mum, Emma and our Stevie will be all alone in the house while we're at shop. What'll they do for their tea?'

Mum laughed again. 'They won't starve,' she said. 'Fridge and freezer packed with enough grub to feed an army. You can rustle up stuff, can't you, Emma?'

I nodded, thinking, Don't let Stevie near the fridge! It'd look as if a swarm of locusts had gone through it.

'That's settled, then,' said Mum. When Dad opened his mouth, Mum added before he could say anything, 'If Emma looks like she's dying from exhaustion or they're both starving to death, we'll think again.'

We all laughed, but Dad had to add his two-penn'orth.

'There'll be homework to do, Emma. You'll do it after your tea?'

''Course I will,' I said.

I believed I would and all. So we left it at that.

I was very glad my mum was thinking the way she did. Dad was inclined to fuss, but she had more trust in me, I thought. 'Spread your wings a bit,' she'd said to me, and that's what it felt like. I wasn't a little kid.

I'd been spending some time over the summer with Joanne, a girl who lived just down the road, and no way was she a little kid either. She was only a few months older than me, but she could have passed for sixteen, easy. She was a big girl, tall and fat, and she had boobs, which was more than I had. I had to admit that compared to Joanne I still looked like a little kid. I was very happy to hang out with someone who seemed a lot older.

We hadn't been special friends at juniors, in fact Joanne didn't have that many friends. You know how some kids at school always seem to get left out, they're just not part of a gang? That never worried me, being in a gang. I always got on okay with the other kids. But Joanne was always hanging about on the edge of things, never really part of anything. Some kids took the mickey out of her, not just as she was fat, but also because her front teeth stuck out a bit, just asking for all the Bugs Bunny remarks. I wondered why she didn't have them fixed – a lot of kids wore braces – but I didn't want to hurt her feelings. She could be sharp with her tongue, and that made people not like her. But she was always fine to me, and during that summer holiday, when we were both at home, we saw more and more of each other.

Joanne wasn't sharp with me. In fact she was flattering. 'Oh, I wish I were slim like you, Emma,' she'd say. 'I wish I had curly hair like yours.' Her hair was mousy-brown, thin and dead straight, and she hated it. What I liked about Joanne was, she was upfront. She did speak her mind, and I admired that. I wished I could do it. She never seemed to care if she offended anyone. She was outgoing, she had confidence, she was bold, she'd talk back.

She also had a lot of other things that I had no way of knowing about. And to this day I don't know whether she actually planned anything from the start. I hope not.

The first couple of years at comp were everything I'd been hoping for. There was a whole lot more going on than at juniors. The place itself was enormous, half a dozen separate buildings spread out, with playgrounds and sports fields attached. It was a right route march to get from one lesson to another – but I liked that. I'd got bored stuck in one classroom all the time, mostly with one teacher, and now it was all part of the new experience. I was happy joining the masses of kids of all ages rushing between the buildings, clutching their books and stuff, seeing a different teacher for each lesson. Every hour of the day was different. It made me feel part of a big, important thing, part of growing up.

The oldest kids at school really did look grown-up, seeing as how they were sixteen or so. The girls more than the boys, though – most of the boys seemed much younger, somehow. Like my brother Stevie and his friends. They might have been in the top class, but they often seemed like little kids, tearing all over the place, being noisy and mucking about. No harm in them, though. It was just that the girls seemed more together, more adult, more neatly dressed. And that's what I was aiming for too.

As my old head teacher had thought, I got on fine with the work. It was tougher than at juniors, but I found it all very interesting, especially English and maths. I was in set 1 for English, and set 2 for maths. (The sets were 1 to 5, with 1 the highest and 5 the lowest.) From the off, I brought back good reports, with straight As – my mum and dad were right chuffed. Even sports couldn't spoil it for me. I've never been sporty, myself, but I could swim and run fast, and I got by. All in all I was in my element.

Mum never had to call me in the morning to get up. While she'd be going, 'Stevie! Stevie! Get a move on, lad!' I'd be up and about already, eager to start the day.

Friends helped, of course. In those first years, they were more and more important. There were so many kids at the school, around 3,000, that it was good to have your own group that you belonged to. I always thought that if you were one of those poor kids who couldn't make friends, or who were always laughed at, school must have been a very lonely place. I was lucky, and had a good group of friends. I'd known them all from juniors.

There were five of us: me, Joanne who I've mentioned before, Chloe, Sophie and Claire. We were a mixed bunch, right enough. It was a bit like a family – when people look at sisters and say, 'Oh, she's the clever one,' or 'She's the good-looking one.' Like they're putting kids in little boxes.

Joanne, as I've said, was big and loud and determined. You could call her the ringleader, except that the rest of us wouldn't have stood for being pushed around. It was more like she thought of cool things to do and swept us along. Chloe was more like me, being quieter, and smaller. She stood out by being really pretty, with beautiful red hair that rippled down to her shoulders in waves, and enormous blue-green eyes. Looked as if butter wouldn't melt – but she had her naughty side, liked to take risks. Sophie was dark, with soft brown eyes and dark brown hair, cut short. A bit on the chubby side, which never seemed to bother her. 'I like me food too much,' she'd say with a grin, always good for a laugh. Claire – well, Claire didn't stand out particularly. She was just reliable and good-natured, nice to be with, never said a bad word about anyone.

Of course, there was a lot more to each of us than what I've said, but that was us in a nutshell. All of us lived on the estate except Chloe. She lived with her mum and her sister Laura in a little house in the village.

There was another thing about friends. As I was getting older – well, we all were – the best thing in life was being with your mates, just hanging out, much more than being at home. It's not that I was cutting myself off from my family, far from it, but I had so much in common with these girls, we were on the same wavelength. We talked about anything and everything – school, boys, TV, music – and we always had a good laugh, that was the very best bit. We'd get together at break time and in the dinner hour, and walking to school and back. Despite Dad's fears,

I wasn't worn out walking nearly two miles a day. Auntie Sue did offer to give me a lift, and it was very kind of her, like always, but I liked to go off with my mates.

We'd arrange to meet up after school somewhere. We'd go home and change out of uniform, then go to one or another's house, or walk down to the village and mooch around the shops and maybe hang out at the park. I never had any interest in clubs or societies or any organised after-school activities. Stevie, now, joined anything he could sign his name to – Scouts especially. Mum would say to me, 'Don't you fancy Guides, Emma?' and I'd just shake my head. My friends were the only company I wanted.

I suppose if you'd asked me then what I was going to do with myself in the future, I would have said something like, 'Um, GCSEs, A levels, maybe university' – though that time seemed ages away. Mum and Dad were very keen on me getting a proper education.

'You mark my words,' said Dad on more than one occasion. 'You need education in this life. If you get a good education you can do anything you put your mind to.'

He hadn't been one for college himself, first off, and neither had Mum, but later they'd both got qualifications and landed good jobs.

'There's a lot of competition now, Emma,' Mum would say. 'If you want to get a good job, you have to have right bits of paper.'

But as I say, getting a job seemed a long way off. Though when I was thirteen – a teenager at last – I had a taste of paid work. And I can't say I took to it.

'You're old enough to help out now, Emma,' said Dad. 'We're not asking for much, though. Just Friday evenings, six till nine, while me and your mum are at wholesalers.'

'Wholesalers, yeah,' I said.

'Oh all right, we'll pop into pub for a pie and a pint after. Nice to have time on us own.'

That was true. Mum and Dad worked such long hours, they hardly had any time off, and what they did have had to be worked out in advance. And the pub would have been a special treat. They drank wine and beer at home at mealtimes, but not a lot.

So I walked to the shop after school, and had tea with my nan, who was still living in the flat above. Now that was a treat, for a weekday. She'd always do me a roast – beef, Yorkshire pud, thick gravy, the works – and it was grand. Stevie would be out with his mates somewhere, and as I told him, he didn't know what he was missing. Sometimes Auntie Sue would join us, if she wasn't going out with her own mates. She saw a lot of her mum, but at this time she still had her own flat in the village.

But then came six o'clock, and with a full belly I'd plod downstairs to join Joanie, the woman who helped Mum and Dad. She was working here just about full-time now, as business was good. She was great, Joanie, really kind, usually with a smile on her sharp little face, her dark permed hair sticking out all round like a halo. As I was sat there on a stool, unpacking stuff and ticking it off on long lists, before stacking it on the shelves, I must have had a face like a wet weekend, it was so boring. Joanie would take pity on me. When it got to seven o'clock, she'd say, 'You leave that, love. I'll finish off. You pop up and see your nan.'

I was off like a shot. It became a routine. Seven o'clock, me and Nan were tucked up in front of *Emmerdale*. Seven-thirty: *Coronation Street*. Eight o'clock: *EastEnders*. She'd always have snacks handy in case we got peckish, and bottles of pop. Then at eight-thirty, time to go down to the shop again, and do my bit. I'd work the till sometimes, though I wasn't supposed to serve cigarettes or alcohol. Thinking about it, I can't say I earned my ten quid. I could have sat there reading the magazines and eating choccie bars till the cows came home, and Mum and Dad would have been none the wiser. I squared it in my mind by thinking I was keeping Nan company, and I did make myself a bit useful.

But if you think that's not giving value for money, you should have seen my brother Stevie. Before he left the comp he had a weekend paper round – of a sort.

'Other boys manage to get round on their bikes,' I said to him, taking the mickey. 'What do you do? Get a lift!'

That's right. Auntie Sue would call for him first thing in the morning on a Saturday and Sunday, they'd go to the shop and pick up the papers to deliver. Mum or Dad would have been marking them up. They only did deliveries at the weekend.

'You spoil that boy,' Mum and Dad would say. But Auntie Sue always laughed, a real good sport.

What none of us knew for quite a while was that Stevie didn't even get off his arse to post the papers through the letterboxes. Auntie Sue did it! While he was sat in the car, keeping his strength up with Mars bars, she was the one walking up and down the front paths.

What a pair, me and Stevie. Didn't look like we'd live up to Mum and Dad's ideas about working hard for a living. Still, we were just schoolkids, I suppose. And to give him his due, Stevie did have his sights set on a career, and he was dead serious.

'I'm gonna work on oil rigs, me,' he announced one day.

Mum and Dad took this in their own ways.

'It'll be the making of him,' said Dad.

'It'll be the dying of him,' Mum shot back. I knew she'd be thinking of the dangers at sea, the storms, the disasters you read about in the papers.

But we all knew that Stevie was a natural for the job. He was a very active, physical kind of lad, practical, good with his hands, and he wasn't cut out for sitting still behind a desk.

'I want to learn a trade,' he said, 'and earn good money.'

Fair enough. I think Mum and Dad were proud of him really, for knowing his own mind, setting his heart on an ambition and actually doing something about it instead of sitting around and thinking the world owed him a living. According to Dad, there were far too many young folk doing that already.

You can't work on an oil rig till you're eighteen, Stevie told us, so when he left school at sixteen – which was my first year at comp – he spent the next two years at the college in town, learning stuff like welding to get him in with a better chance of the job he wanted. The day he got a letter offering him an interview, you could hear him whooping streets away. Then when he got the job…well, you could've heard him in the next village. All his hard work had paid off, and he'd be starting some time in early November.

We were all glad for him, of course, despite the fact we'd all miss him to bits. Me and Mum especially got upset thinking about all the dangers, but Stevie wasn't having any of it.

'I'll be well trained,' he said. 'It's the best in the world, bar none.'

I'm not sure that made us feel any better.

It's a funny thing, looking back. It's like the pieces of a jigsaw falling into place. You're not at all aware of the pieces at the time, or that there's any pattern to fill up in the first place. It's only later that you can see that there are pieces, and they do fit.

Stevie going away was one of the pieces, and so was my mum and dad working all hours. I was left a lot on my own, but to me that was a good thing. Showed I was really growing up, a proper independent teenager. A lot of my friends had parents who were out at work all day. What harm could come to me? I wasn't stupid, far from it. And I'd been told time and again through my life what dangers to look out for.

'Don't take sweets from strangers.'

'Never get in a strange man's car. Even if he knows your name, if you don't know who he is, don't get in the car. Run away.'

Yes, Mum and Dad had drilled it into me, how to stay safe. Better safe than sorry. Use your mobile if you're the least bit worried. Call us any time and we'll come and get you. Of course they would.

I had this image in my mind of a dirty old man. He really would be dirty and old, wearing stained clothes, unshaven, probably with teeth missing. He'd try and lure me into his clapped-out old van. He'd be absolutely disgusting. He was part of that dark and dangerous world out there, where a rapist would leap out at you from the bushes if you took a short cut in the dark. Where prostitutes hung around on street corners, dirty women, wearing short skirts that showed their stocking tops and low-cut blouses that showed most of their boobs. They'd do sex for money, and that was disgusting too. They had minders, called pimps, and they were all gangsters who carried knives and probably guns as well. Then there were the druggies – pathetic, skin-and-bone wrecks, white-faced and trembling, no use to anyone but a danger when they had to steal money for a fix.

No way would I be involved in that horrible world. It couldn't touch me. I didn't need Mum and Dad's advice, I could look after myself.

But that was before I learned that there's such a thing as disguise. Bad things don't have to look bad. In fact they can look good. Very good.

4

My Second Home

'But what d'you *do* all day?' asked Dad. He wasn't kidding, he really couldn't get his head round it.

Me and Mum looked at each other and laughed. Dad never understood the idea of shopping. If he wanted to buy anything, it was get in, look round, choose what you want, and out. No idea about window shopping, see what's around, think about it all before making a decision. As far as I was concerned, you didn't even have to actually buy anything to have a good time – and right now my best times were at the big shopping mall a bus ride away.

I'd known the mall for ever. Mum and Dad used to take us kids there when we were little. For ordinary everyday shopping there was Morrisons or Tesco in the nearest town, but for anything special – clothes, presents, whatever – it had to be the mall. Not that I'd ever thought of making a day of it. That had been

Joanne's idea, all us girls hanging out there together of a Saturday.

'I mean, you're thirteen, Emma,' she'd said to me just after my last birthday. 'Your mum and dad'll let you stay out now, won't they?'

Well, they did, though Dad insisted on laying down the law.

'I want you girls to stay together,' he said. 'No wandering off alone, okay?'

It was nearly always me, Joanne and Chloe spending the day together, but Sophie and Claire made it when they could. I liked it best when we were all together – we really had a vibe. But of course it was still good when it was just me, Joanne and Chloe.

Dad's other rule was getting the five-forty-five bus back home – 'No later, mind.'

I didn't mind. The shops shut at five-thirty, so there wouldn't be much to stay for. Anyway, as we'd arrive about ten-thirty in the morning, that meant we'd have around seven hours to ourselves. Plenty of time to wander round the shops, see what was new, try on stuff we had no intention of buying, and squirt perfume from tester bottles in Boots. Plenty of time to stop for a Coke in one of the little cafés, or sit on a bench eating sweets we bought in the Italian shop, which was best for ice cream as well as sweets. We'd have our dinner in McDonald's, usually, burger and chips, sitting on one of the balconies and watching the world go by, hundreds of people, even thousands, as we gossiped about this and that, or criticised other girls' clothes...

For a change, we'd wander outside, if the sun was shining, and I remember it shining a lot that summer. There were gardens all round the place, with grass and lots of trees and bushes and flowers. You could usually find a private place to sit. It was nice, like having a picnic. It was like being in the country – or as near to the country as I ever wanted to get. I'm a proper town person, me. I might have grown up in a village, but it's towns for me. I'd been on trips to the country as a kid and couldn't see the point. No shops, too much space, too quiet, nothing to do. But it's pretty, I give you that, and I like to look at it from a distance. In those days, as far as I was concerned, the best place to look at the rolling hills on the horizon was from just outside the mall.

And inside, there was yet another attraction – an amusement arcade. Not like the big flash ones I went to at Blackpool, but still a proper arcade, a separate section tucked away on the first floor, surrounded by a wooden fence. I suppose the idea was to keep the really little kids out, in case they were scared by all the noise and lights. It had the usual shoot-'em-up games, the racing cars, the fruit machines, but more than anything I liked the dance machine. You put your money in and the music belted out, while arrows on the floor lit up, showing you where to put your feet. Fantastic! You could kid yourself you were on TV, some reality talent show. We all loved it.

I was into really good music now. I felt a bit embarrassed to think there'd been a time I actually liked the Spice Girls and Boyzone, bought their discs and watched them on telly. Still, mustn't be too hard on myself, I was only a kid, and pop music like that is meant for kids. Now I liked something with more to it, more guts, like hip-hop and R&B, and the dance machine was great for that. I poured pounds into it. I must have spent more on that than on clothes. Magic.

I'd never have gone to the mall by myself. It wasn't that I thought anything bad would happen to me (though I'm sure Dad thought it would, if I didn't go about in a posse). It was just that everything was more fun when you could share it with your mates. I would've enjoyed it even if it wasn't such a fabulous place to be. Everybody loved it. Well, except my nan. A year or two back, Mum had persuaded her to come with us one afternoon. 'Very grand,' Nan admitted, looking at the sheer size of it, the pillars going up and up and the balconies on each floor and the hundreds of shops of all sorts. 'But I'll stick to market, if you don't mind.'

That was in our local town, the market. I went with her sometimes, and I can't say I liked it. It was old-fashioned, rickety stalls with tatty awnings, but that's not what turned me off. Not only were you out in the open air and got wet when it rained, but there was always a horrible smell hanging around, as if something had gone off – manky meat. Nan swore blind that it was the best place to buy meat, and of course she wouldn't buy anything that was off. You only had to taste her roasts to know it was first class. But still...there wasn't a lot in the market that would keep me for long. Apart from the smell, the clothes stalls just sold tat, cheap tat, T-shirts for a pound, that sort of thing. Makes me sound snobby, I know, but it didn't have class.

The mall, now...it was like it got to be my home from home. When I wasn't there I was wishing I was, and when I was there, I was making the most of it. I got to know it so well I could see pictures in my head of all the shops, what they were and where they were, and all the places to eat, on each level.

But as I say, the whole mall wouldn't have meant

much to me without my mates. Sometimes we'd meet other people we knew, friends from school or neighbours from the village. Always time for a chat. Joanne especially seemed to know a lot of people – she was forever being stopped by someone or other. She even seemed to know some of the security guards by name. After a while I realised it was mostly boys who said, 'Hi, Joanne.' But there didn't seem anything in it. None of us girls had what you'd call a boyfriend, though there was lots of talk at school about who fancied who, all that sort of thing. Some girls in my class boasted about their boyfriends, but I never knew how much truth there was in it. Me, I wasn't bothered, not a bit. Maybe I was a late developer, boyfriend-wise, but it never crossed my mind to think of a boy in that way. Like with Stevie's mates, I was happy just to be friends. So when Joanne took to introducing me to some boys she knew, that's what I thought. Friends – new friends.

The first two lads were called Niv and Jay. I was sat on a bench getting my breath back after having a go on the dance machine. Chloe and Sophie were with me, and Joanne had gone off to get some Coke for us all. She came back with more than the Coke. We saw her walking back towards us with a lad either side of her.

'Hiya,' Joanne called out as she got up to us, taking out bottles of Coke from a plastic bag and handing them out. As we opened them, Joanne pointed at one of the boys. 'This is Niv,' she said. 'And this is his cousin Jay,' pointing at the other. Then she waved a hand at us and ran all our names together: 'ChlocEmmaSophie.'

The boys smiled, and we smiled back.

They looked friendly, the boys. They stayed standing with Joanne while the rest of us stayed sat on the bench. I realised this was the first time I'd actually spoken direct to an Asian lad – or any Asian person, come to that. I didn't know then if they were Indian or Pakistani, and wasn't sure of the difference anyway. What I was aware of, straight away, was how nice they looked. That made a real impact.

I don't mean that I fancied them there and then. As I've said, I wasn't ready for that kind of thing yet. I just liked the way they looked – very clean and neat. Their skin was a lovely warm light brown colour, like honey, very smooth, and their eyes were very dark brown with long curling lashes. Their thick black hair was glossy, styled in a natural kind of way. Their teeth were really white, and even. As they were talking, I couldn't help noticing their hands. Their fingernails were immaculate, totally clean and manicured. From what they were saying, about school and exams, the boys must have been the same age as us, thirteen or fourteen, but they were a world away from the boys in my class. The boys I was used to were mostly mucky pups, hair all over the place, fingernails filthy with God knows what, their faces covered in spots which they made worse by scratching. They never bothered about their clothes, either. Shirts usually grubby, trousers all creased and shoes scuffed.

These boys here in the mall really could have come from another planet, one where lads cared about their personal appearance – and hygiene. Their clothes were top quality, I could tell. They wouldn't have got their T-shirts and jeans from a pound shop in Nan's market, that's for sure, and their trainers were genuine designer, not rip-offs.

The way they spoke was different too. I don't mean the accent, which was the same as ours. I mean they weren't noisy, or show-off. They laughed, but not loudly, not trying to get attention. And there was none of the annoying joshing a lot of boys went in for – flicking your hair or poking your arm or making rude comments. I suppose I'm saying they were just more grown up, more like sophisticated young men than rough-and-tumble schoolboys. All I know is that I was very struck, and very admiring.

Part of what I liked was the fact they were unusual,

being Asian. In our part of the world, in those days you just didn't see people from the ethnic minorities every day. The villages and small towns hereabouts had always been nothing but white, so people grew up living next door to people like themselves, and working with them too. Even our huge comprehensive school only had a couple of black or brown kids. It's different in the cities, of course, where immigrants tend to go and live and work first off. For people like me, though, these boys were different – but in a good way. And I've always liked what's new and interesting. They were fascinating, with their good looks and their charm.

Now they were getting ready to leave. I for one felt we'd had a real friendly chat. 'Nice meeting you,' they said with a wave. 'See you next week?'

'Sure.' We all nodded and waved back as they walked towards the escalator.

When they were out of sight, Chloe said, 'They're nice. Where did you meet them, Joanne?'

Joanne just shrugged and said, 'Oh, you know, around.'

We never did find out.

I know you have to be careful when it comes to talking about different races. People can get very prickly if they think you're being racist. I like to think there's never been a racist bone in my body. Why should there be? I can honestly say that it never even crossed my mind to look down on Asian people, or anyone else. I could see there were some differences, in the way people dressed, for instance. In Leeds on a visit I'd see women wearing brightly coloured clothes, saris, and thought they looked gorgeous. I wasn't too sure about the long black robes some women wore, that covered them up from head to foot. I would have felt suffocated. But still, it was their choice, their way of life. It was as natural to them as wearing jeans and trainers and T-shirts was for me.

So that was the thing, as far as I was concerned. People were different, not better or worse. And the differences just made life more interesting.

I never bothered my head about different religions, either. I wasn't religious myself, and nor was my family, so that was never an issue. Whenever there was anything on the news about religious or racial problems, or both, my dad would say, 'Why don't they just live and let live?'

At home, there was none of that talk I'd heard in some of my friends' houses, about 'They come over here, take our jobs, take our houses...' As my dad said, 'If they come here to work, they pay taxes, they look after their families, what's wrong with that?'

Nan wasn't so sure. You'd hear her grumble about 'blacks' now and then, if there was something on the news on telly. But as Dad said, that was more about being old and out of touch. 'As folk get older,' he said to me, 'they get set in their ways, they don't like change. And she's never even known a black or Asian person, not properly, so she doesn't know we're all the same, really.'

So no, my story, what happened to me, was never about race. It was about men, and crime.

After that first Saturday, which was some time in the middle of June, we met up with Niv and Jay every week, till it got like a routine. Us girls would get to the mall, do our own thing, and sooner or later the boys would turn up and join us. We'd hang out in the arcade, play games, have a go on the dance machine, all the usual kind of stuff. Sometimes we'd go outside, take a walk. We'd be sat on the grass, chilling out, away from other people.

It was always Joanne who spotted the boys first, I remember. I'm not sure if she was actually keeping an eye out for them. Maybe she could just see further than the rest of us as she was so tall!

The weeks turned into months, and it was like we'd known these two boys for ever, even if we only ever saw them on Saturdays. It's not like they singled any of us out. We all chatted together. And it wasn't chatting up. It was just talking to each other about things we liked – music, films, TV, even some school stuff. In fact it was about school the first time me and Niv had a really long chat. The autumn term had started, so it must have been in September. I was moaning about maths, of all things.

'It's this new teacher,' I told him. 'She's a right cow. I used to like maths, me, but she's gone and spoiled it.'

'What does she do, then?' Niv asked.

'Oh, you know, she's all sarky, takes the mickey out of you if you can't answer straight off.'

'I know what you mean,' said Niv. He was being really sympathetic, really took an interest in what I was saying.

This was new to me. Most boys I knew couldn't wait to start talking about themselves, they didn't show much interest in what you might be saying, or feeling. And they usually brought the talk round to football before long, like my brother Stevie.

I told Niv about Stevie and his plans, too.

'An oil rig?' he said. 'That's brave. You wouldn't catch me out at sea in a storm.'

'Oh, he's getting all proper training,' I told him. 'It's not like he'll just be chucked in at deep end.'

'Did he always want to work on a rig?' Niv asked.

'Yeah…well, it were that or summat to do with motors,' I said. Stevie was mad on cars and how they worked, always tinkering with the engine on Dad's car. He was having driving lessons now, and hoped to pass his test before he went away. That was another thing most boys were interested in – cars. But here was Niv, quite happy to hear about my problems at school and about my family.

'What does your dad do?' he asked.

So I told him about the shop, and how Mum worked there too.

'They must work all hours,' he said.

'Yeah. They don't get home till gone nine.'

He whistled. 'That's a long day. Do you come back to an empty house, then?'

'Yeah – or I will when Stevie leaves.'

'When's that?'

'Coupla months.'

'Don't you mind being on your own?' he went on.

''Course not,' I shot back. As if I was a little kid. 'Anyway, I'm not on my own. I usually meet up with Joanne or Chloe or the others.'

'Do your own thing?'

'Yeah, that's right,' I said, and grinned. 'We go to us houses, or hang around in village.'

'That must be really exciting,' he said with a laugh.

As if. Our village wasn't the most happening place in the universe. When he'd asked me where I lived, Niv had never heard of it, so I had to describe just where it was, and where our estate was. He even wanted to know how long it took me to walk home from the bus stop.

'Where do you live?' I asked Niv.

'Leeds,' he said. That would fit, I thought. Big city. I felt a twinge of envy, all that interesting stuff on your doorstep, cool shops and stuff. And gigs – when I was fourteen, I'd be going to proper gigs with my friends, without Mum or Dad.

Now Niv was gathering his things together.

'I'd better go,' he said. 'Nice talking to you, Emma.'

'You too,' I said.

Then a thought seemed to strike him.

'Tell you what,' he said. 'About that maths thing. I'm pretty good at maths, though I say it meself. If you're ever stuck, call me.'

He fished out a piece of paper from his pocket and scribbled his number on it.

'Cheers,' I said. It seemed polite to give him my number in return, so I wrote it on another piece of paper he gave me.

'Great,' Niv said, and with a quick smile that

showed off his perfect white teeth, he strolled over to Jay, who was sitting at a table with Joanne and Chloe, and tapped him on the shoulder. Jay got up, and they both made their way out, waving their goodbyes.

I was left thinking how thoughtful Niv was, how kind. There was just a hint of flattery in there too, I thought. He'd certainly gone out of his way to talk to me, and seemed really interested. But just in a friendly way. And to think he'd even offered to help me with my maths... What a star. In a funny way he reminded me of my auntie Sue. She's always been interested in people, but because she's kind, not nosy. She wants to know what makes them tick, what they think and how they feel. She's a big-hearted person; she really relates to everyone she meets. Yeah, I said to myself. Niv's like that. Otherwise, why would he want to know so much about me?

5

Going to Town

It dawned on me later that I'd done most of the talking. Niv didn't seem to want to talk about himself, and I put it down to him not being big-headed. Anyway, it didn't matter if I didn't know much about him. He was good company, and it was enough to hang out with him and Jay.

And with a guy called Ali, as it happened. I met this Ali the very next Saturday in the mall. I was there with Joanne and Chloe, sitting in McDonald's, when we heard, 'Hi, girls!' It was Niv, coming up to our table with Jay and another lad. No, not a lad. This one was older, maybe late teens, early twenties, it was hard to tell. A young man rather than a boy, anyway.

'You don't know Ali, do you?' Niv said to me and Chloe, and we shook our heads, smiling. After all, any friend of theirs...

'Pleased to meet you,' said Ali, holding out his hand.

'And you've met Joanne,' Niv went on, waving a hand at her. Ali and Joanne nodded at each other, smiling, very pleasant.

All three of them pulled up chairs and sat at our table.

'Sorry we can't stay for long,' Niv said. 'Big family do this evening. We've gotta go round buying a heap of stuff.'

That's a pity, I thought, but they stayed long enough for me to get a good look at this new arrival.

Like Niv and Jay he was very smart, very well dressed, but where they were casual, he was more kind of formal. He was wearing a well-cut dark suit, with a creamy white shirt, open at the neck, showing a thick gold chain. His black shoes were polished, gleaming. His dark hair was swept back off his face, and his hands were very well kept, with neatly mani-cured nails. There was a big gold signet ring on one of his little fingers. It looked heavy, and pretty classy. All told, he could have stepped out of the pages of a magazine, no trouble. Advertising something posh like champagne or expensive aftershave.

After about ten minutes, Ali pushed up the sleeve of his sharp jacket and looked at his watch – a fancy gold one, which for all I knew could have been a genuine Rolex. 'Sorry, lads, gotta be going. You still want your ride?'

'Yeah,' the two boys said at once, and stood up.

'Sorry we have to be off,' said Niv. 'We'll just have to tear ourselves away from you.'

'And we're gonna get so much stuff, we'll need a lift,' added Jay.

'Oh,' said Chloe. 'You got a car, then, Ali?'

Joanne made the noise that sounds like 'Doh!' And added, 'Watch out, Chloe, you're so sharp you'll cut yourself. Of course he's got a car – a beemer, in't it, Ali?'

Ali looked pleased with himself, I thought. 'Yeah,' he said. 'Wouldn't be without my wheels.'

Then he turned to the boys and said, 'Come on, then, if you're coming.' To us girls he smiled all round and said, 'It was very good to meet you, Emma and Chloe. And to see you again, Joanne. I hope we'll all see each other again soon.' As he spoke he looked straight into the eyes of each of us.

Nice manners. And with a wave they strolled off towards the escalator. At the top, Niv turned round and called out, 'See you next week!'

We waved back and watched them disappear downwards.

'Well!' said Chloe. 'He's a bit of all right, in't he?'

'Which one?' I asked.

Chloe grinned. 'Ali, of course.'

I turned to Joanne. 'How do you know this Ali, then?' I asked her.

She shot me a quick look. 'Why shouldn't I know him?' she said, a bit sharp.

I blinked in surprise. Joanne was getting a bit out of order, there. No need to snap at me.

'Oh, if you must know, I met him the other night,' she said. 'When you and Chloe'd gone off to your little youth club.'

She sounded sharp again, sarky, which I didn't think was fair. She knew why me and Chloe had gone there. We didn't really want to, but my mum and dad had been going on at me to do something in the evenings.

'You're forever hanging about with your mates, Emma,' Dad had said. 'I don't know what you get up to, wandering about. Why don't you go to that new youth club in the village?'

God, he was talking to me as if I was a little kid. Why should he know what I was getting up to – if anything? He forgot I was nearly thirteen and a half, a proper teenager, not at junior school now, having to be looked after. Why couldn't he keep up?

It was Mum who put a different spin on it. 'Well, love,' she said to me. ''Course you like being with your friends, but I've heard they've got a lot going on in the club. You never know, you might like it. Give it a go.'

Oh well, I thought, if it stops them nagging. I'll go just the once. I asked Joanne, but she had just laughed and said, 'Well, if you want to hang out with little kids and play ping-pong...'

Chloe was quite happy to come with me. 'I'll try anything once, me,' she said.

So on the Thursday evening we met up in the village and walked into this old barn-type building near the church. Well, I was glad Joanne wasn't around to say, 'I told you so.' It was all pretty run-down. So much for new! I reckon they'd got a job lot of old chairs and tables from a jumble sale to fill up the place. There was a pin table in a corner, but one of the old ones, not like the swish computerised ones in the mall. Through an open door we could see a small room leading off the main one, where some kids were playing pool. There was a ping-pong table too, though no one was using it.

There were about a dozen other kids in the main room, mooching about, chatting. They'd glanced at me and Chloe when we came in, then went on with what they were doing. They looked younger than us, and I didn't recognise any of them. On top of all this, there was a funny smell, like manky old socks. How could Mum and Dad think this was a good idea?

As we walked out, I said, 'God, what a dump.'

Chloe laughed, then a few steps further on she stopped and said, 'You know what?'

'What?'

'This club, we could use it.'

'Use it? Are you kidding? I wouldn't be seen dead in a place like that.'

'Nah, that's not what I mean. I mean, we could use it.'

'No good, Chloe, I don't know what you're on about.'

'Well,' she said. 'It's what all the oldies like, mums and dads, in't it? Can't get up to owt in a youth club. If they asked, we could always say we were going there...'

The penny dropped.

'Like an alibi!' I said. I hadn't seen cop shows on telly for nothing.

'You what?' said Chloe.

'You know,' I said. 'Saying you were off somewhere when you were really somewhere else and you don't want folk to know.'

'Yeah. Be a laugh, wouldn't it?'

I don't know what made her think of that. It wasn't as if we were going anywhere we shouldn't. But by the time I'd walked home I could see what she meant. It could be a laugh, to pull the wool over Mum and Dad's eyes.

The memory made me smile, and now I said to Joanne, 'You don't know what you missed!'

'Yeah well,' she said, 'bet I were having a better time than you.'

That was probably true. 'Where were you?' I asked.

Joanne scowled. 'In town.'

'That dump?' I had a quick picture in my head of the smelly old market with the pong of rotten meat hanging about. Not where you'd expect to see classy Ali.

'Just shows what you know,' said Joanne. 'There's plenty of places if you know where to look. We had a great time. He took me out in his beemer,' she added with a grin, and nodded, as if she was enjoying the memory.

I could see she was impressed, but didn't recognise the name. I knew she'd take the piss, but I asked anyway.

'What's a beemer?'

Sure enough, Joanne fixed me with a look that said, 'What are you like?' and said, 'Bee. Em. Doubleyou.'

Oh. I'd heard of that. A fancy car, expensive. I'd heard Stevie and Dad talk about BMWs.

Chloe was going on. 'He must be loaded, then. Wonder what he does for a living.'

Joanne looked thoughtful. 'I wonder,' she said. There was a little smile playing round her mouth.

I really was struck by this Ali. To tell the truth, it wasn't so much him, as what he looked like. The kind of life he must live. Whatever he did for a living, he must have started very young to be so well off now. Bet he didn't slave at school for years, then college, I thought to myself.

Mum and Dad had always drilled it into me that I had to have an education, to work hard if I wanted to get anywhere, get a good job, make good money. And fair enough, that seemed okay to me. I understood it, and I was still keeping my end up at school, still got As and very good reports. But maybe this Ali had got where he was, got this glamorous life, without going through all that... Maybe I'd find out how he did it later on. My guess was he'd have to be in something glamorous, like showbiz. I couldn't imagine him in an office, sat at a desk all day looking at computers. Or in a shop, working the till. I had a sudden image of him behind the counter in my dad's shop. The picture made me smile. It was as likely as my dad strutting his stuff on the catwalk. Great male model he'd make!

I hoped I'd see Ali again – maybe he'd be hanging out with his cousins again next Saturday. But as it happened I saw him sooner than that, thanks to Joanne.

We were walking down the road to school on Monday morning when she said, 'Sorry I were a bit sharp the other day. I wanna make it up to you. Why don't you come to town with me this week?'

She must have seen the look on my face, as she laughed and said, 'You're so bloody snobby, Emma! It's not all crap. There's good places to go – and good things to do. You'll see.'

Well, why not? I thought, and nodded. 'Okay, you're on.'

'Let's say tomorrow, then,' said Joanne.

So there we were at six o'clock on a wet Tuesday evening in town. As soon as we'd got off the bus my heart sank. The place looked bad enough when the sun was shining. When it was drizzling with rain, and starting to get dark – well, I've been in more cheerful places. Like a cemetery, I felt like saying to Joanne.

There weren't many people around, not even in the McDonald's where we had our tea. After, we walked round, looking in shop windows. Load of tat. The stalls in the market were closing up as we walked past, but the horrible smell was still floating around.

It wasn't long till I'd had enough, and told Joanne so.

'No,' she said back. 'Just wait a minute. We're nearly there.'

Oh, I thought. Are we actually going somewhere, not just traipsing about these boring streets for the fun of it? So I plodded on beside her. It might have been more fun if Chloe was there – it took a lot to dampen her spirits. But she was off school with a bad cold.

Then Joanne said, 'Right, this is it.'

What's it, I wondered. Just another street, by the look of it, a mix of houses and little shops. More trees along here, though. We were about halfway up it when we heard a beep. It was someone sounding a car horn.

'There he is,' said Joanne, taking my arm and pulling me across the road to where a big black car was parked. As we got near it, the light inside went on, and the driver turned round. I recognised him straight away – Ali! That's a turn-up, I thought, and felt right glad. But why hadn't Joanne mentioned we were meeting him?

I didn't have much time to think about this before Ali opened the front passenger door, leaning over the seat.

'Hi, Emma,' he said, smiling that perfect smile. 'Good to see you again. Get in out of the rain.'

I slid into the front seat, while Joanne got in the back. I glanced round to look at her as she settled into her seat, and realised there was someone else sat in the back already.

'This is Naz,' said Ali, nodding at the guy. 'Naz, this is Emma, Joanne's friend.'

'Pleased to meet you,' said this Naz, smiling at me. He was another good-looking bloke, in Ali's league, easy.

'Are you two cousins?' I asked Ali, thinking back to Niv and Jay.

Ali laughed. 'No, we're brothers,' he said. 'Can't you tell?'

That explained it, the likeness. Though Naz was a bit younger than Ali, I thought.

Now Ali was switching off the light, and saying, 'Right, ladies. Where to?'

'I don't mind,' said Joanne. 'Let's just go round and about. You choose.'

Ali started to drive off as me and Joanne put our seatbelts on. This was a treat, I thought. I wasn't crazy about cars like Stevie, but I knew a classy motor when I saw one. So this was a beemer, I thought. You could hardly hear the engine going, it was that soft, purring like a cat, even when Ali speeded up, taking a road out of town. There was a lovely smell of leather, rich leather. Dead classy upholstery here. I settled back in my seat to enjoy the ride.

Ali drove for about ten minutes. I looked at his hands on the wheel, the gold signet ring on his little finger glowing when we passed under a streetlamp. He held the wheel quite lightly, not gripping it madly like some folks do. I could tell he was used to driving, and was pretty confident.

Then we were turning left, through some gates and into a car park. We rolled to a stop under some trees.

'Know where we are, Emma?' asked Joanne.

It took me just a moment to work out where we were. The light was fading fast, and the place looked a bit different from what I remembered. Then – of course! It was the park we used to go to when I was a kid, a few miles from our village, on the way to town. 'God,' I said, 'I haven't been here for ages.'

I realised Ali was offering me a cigarette, from a flat shiny gold box.

'Like one?' he asked.

'Er...' I didn't know what to say. Were they ordinary fags? I had tried some before, and it wasn't bad, but I wasn't sure I did it right. I wouldn't want to choke and splutter and make a fool of myself in front of everyone.

'Yeah, thanks,' Joanne cut in, and leant over between the front seats to take a fag from the box. She took another for Naz, and sat back.

'You don't have to if you don't want to,' said Ali. He was smiling at me, and his eyes looked kind.

'No, you're all right,' I said at once. 'Just takes some getting used to.' And I took a fag out of the box.

Ali did too, then put the box back in his pocket and got out a lighter from another pocket. This lighter was gold, and like his signet ring it looked solid, heavy and expensive. He turned round while Joanne and Naz leaned forward. He lit their fags and they moved back in their seats. Joanne took a drag, breathed out the smoke and went, 'Aaaaah!'

Ali lit my fag, and I drew on it. 'Don't hurry,' he said. 'Take it easy.'

So I went slowly, and managed to finish the fag without choking. I felt a bit light-headed, but not bad. God, Mum and Dad would kill me if they saw me smoking! Mum was a smoker herself, but she always said she wished she'd never started. 'Don't you start, Emma,' she'd say. 'You'll get hooked and then you'll regret it for the rest of your life, like I do.' She was forever trying to stop, but never managed it. Used to drive her mad. Dad, on the other hand, had never smoked, and he hated it. At home, Mum had to smoke outside in the garden or in the little utility room at the back of the house if it was cold or wet outside.

I noticed the windows had wound down smoothly, without a sound. The others had flipped their dog ends out, so I did the same.

'Give us a drink, Ali,' Joanne was saying. Ali opened the glove compartment and brought out a bottle of vodka. I recognised the label – Smirnoff. Mum and Dad had a bottle in the cabinet at home, but they weren't great spirit drinkers. That bottle had been there for years. I'd never tried it, but I'd heard it was good.

Joanne was glugging straight from the bottle. Not very hygienic, I thought. I was surprised Ali hadn't produced proper glasses from somewhere. Then Joanne wiped her mouth and passed the bottle to me. I didn't want to offend her by wiping the top too obviously – she was bound to say something like, 'Think I'll poison you, do you?' So I turned round to sit straight, and out of her sight quickly wiped the bottle with my hankie. Then I took a sip, then another. Hmmm. I could feel the liquid moving down my throat, into my stomach and into my guts. It didn't taste of much, but a warm feeling went through me, and I just sat there, holding the bottle till Ali said, 'Have some more, Emma.'

I won't say I glugged it, but I took a proper mouthful and swallowed it down. The warm feeling got even better, so I had another. This made me gasp, and by now my head was feeling a bit funny, kind of floating. I'd never been drunk – was this what it was like? Well, if it was, it wasn't bad at all.

Before I realised it, Ali had taken the bottle from me, and was taking a quick swig. 'Can't have too much,' he said, passing the bottle back to his brother. 'Don't want to be done for drink driving.'

With that, he turned the engine on. 'Better get going,' he said. 'You have to be back by nine, don't you, Emma?'

I nodded. 'Yeah.' Wonder how he knew? But I was getting sleepy, and didn't think any more about it. In fact, before I knew it, Ali was shaking my shoulder and saying, 'Wake up, Emma, you're home.'

I blinked and looked out. It was proper dark now. All the village street lights were on. I managed to open the door and stumbled out. But I didn't forget my manners. 'Thank you for a very nice evening,' I burbled. Ali smiled, and said, 'The first of many, I hope.'

Then Joanne was taking my arm and we were walking up the road. She'd been drinking quite a bit more, by the sound of her. Giggling away. As we reached her gate, she said, 'See, Emma? Don't have to be at mall to have a good time!' And she wandered up her front path.

She's right there, I thought, going on up the street. The cold air had cleared the fug in my head a bit, and I wasn't stumbling so much. Still, I was glad Mum and Dad wouldn't be home yet. I bet they could smell the fag smoke on me, if nothing else.

I got ready for bed quickly. Didn't have the energy even to clean my teeth. I'd get clean properly in the morning. I was that glad to lie down. I didn't feel sick, just a bit woozy. More than that, though, I could feel something else, in the pit of my stomach. Sort of excited, glad. I'd had a fab time this evening. Sitting in a posh car with two good-looking guys, smoking cigarettes and drinking vodka. How cool was that?

And when could I do it again?

6

Join the Club

I didn't have to wait long for my next fix of the good life. Two days, in fact.

On the Wednesday morning, I woke up with a bit of a headache, very unusual for me. I was slow getting ready, I still felt a bit wobbly. But at least a good soak in the bath and a hairwash would get rid of the smell of fag smoke. I knew that if I was going to be doing stuff that Mum and Dad wouldn't approve of, I had to be just the same as usual. And I knew for a fact they wouldn't approve of me going off for a ride in a guy's car, even if Joanne was there too. They'd want to know all about him, check him out. And that was without the smoking and drinking! So – no way would they find out.

Chloe was still off school, but I could tell Sophie and Claire about my adventures. I'd told them about meeting Ali at the mall, and they were all ears. Now I had something even better to tell them. Which I did, at break time. I tried to sound cool, as if driving around in luxury and smoking and drinking wasn't such a big deal, but I bet they weren't fooled. No getting away from it – I was like a kid with a new toy. Sophie went, 'Wow!' as I hoped they both would. But Claire was quiet.

'I don't know, Emma,' she said, frowning a bit. 'It could have been right dangerous.'

'What?' I asked back. 'Having meself a good time?'

'Oh, you know what I mean,' said Claire. 'This Ali, he's a bit older, in't he? Not a lad. And with his brother too. What if he'd tried owt on?'

'Well he didn't!' I fired back. I didn't want her to take the shine off it. And Joanne added, 'I were there too, remember. They weren't gonna try owt on.'

Claire shrugged, and turned away.

'So you won't wanna come with us next time then?' I asked her.

'No,' she said. 'I won't.' And she walked off.

'Oh, take no notice of her,' said Joanne.

'When are you going again?' asked Sophie.

'Dunno...' Joanne shrugged. 'What about Thursday?'

'Fine by me,' I said straight off, and could've kicked myself for sounding like a little kid, all eager.

Sophie's face fell. 'I can't make it.'

'Always another time,' said Joanne, and we left it at that. Me, I couldn't wait for Thursday evening.

'Are we meeting Ali at the same place?' I asked Joanne as we waited in the village for the bus to town.

'No,' she said. 'He's not around tonight.'

Oh. That was a downer. I'd been looking forward to another ride.

'He's got a lot on, you know,' said Joanne. 'Can't always be hanging about for us.'

'Right,' I said, wondering again just what it was that he did for a living. If he was busy this evening, then he didn't keep usual office hours. More like shop hours, I thought. At least, a shop like ours that stayed open late.

'Who'll be there then?' I asked.

Joanne waved her hand, 'Oh, I dunno. There'll be Naz for sure, and maybe some of his mates. Depends.'

She looked straight at me. 'We'll just hang out, okay?'

'Okay,' I said.

At least it wasn't raining when we arrived. 'Which way?' I asked as we left the bus stop.

'Old market,' she said.

What? I thought. The smelly old market? What's she thinking of? The old market wasn't my idea of glamour. I couldn't think it was anyone's idea of glamour.

As it happened, the market had an attraction I never knew about.

Joanne led me round the side of the stalls and past the market house, which was a kind of community centre but not used much. Then down a little alley and round a corner and up to a wooden door in a wall. 'In here,' she said, pushing the door open. It creaked as we stepped through, into a sort of yard. Concrete floor, no roof, brick walls. There was a big iron gate on one side.

As I was taking all this in, I heard my name.

'Emma! Good to see you again!'

It was Naz, coming towards us with a big grin on his face. He nodded to Joanne, and said, 'Welcome to the pleasure palace!'

Yeah, right. Very like a palace. But I cheered up seeing him. He was a friendly face, very welcome. And I could see a couple of figures behind him.

'Come and meet my friends,' he said. 'Hami and Bez, meet Emma.'

We all smiled and said hello. As Naz didn't mention Joanne, they must have known her already.

'What am I thinking?' said Naz. 'I haven't offered you a drink. Come and sit down.'

He waved us towards a couple of wooden benches in a corner, facing each other. As me and Joanne settled ourselves, he was getting a bottle out of a bag on the floor. It was Smirnoff again. Good, I thought. I'd taken to that the other night.

'And look,' Naz was saying. 'Crystal glasses too!' And he waved a couple of paper cups. We laughed, and I couldn't help feeling glad we weren't all going to drink from the same bottle. He poured the drinks, and a couple more for Hami and Bez.

These two hadn't said much apart from hello. They sat on the other bench, perfectly relaxed. They were older than Naz, maybe even older than Ali. Grown men. The light was still good enough for me to see they were as smartly dressed as their friends, in sharp suits, well-polished shoes and all. As they lifted their cups I could see a glint of gold at their wrists. After a few sips, one of them, Bez, put his cup down and offered us cigarettes from a flat gold case. Soon we were all sitting there puffing away and sipping our drinks. I could shut my eyes, I thought, and be in some posh bar.

As the drink went down, the warmth spread through me and I began to feel more comfortable, at ease. I could get used to this.

Naz was saying, 'I could see your face as you came

in, Emma. I knew what you were thinking – "What a dump!" Am I right?'

I smiled. Yeah, he was right, so I nodded.

'I don't blame you,' he said. 'That's what I thought when I first saw it. Not the most beautiful part of town – not that there's much competition.'

Right again.

'The thing is,' he went on. 'It might be what you call basic, but it's got something special. Know what that is?'

I shook my head.

'It's private,' he said. 'Not many people know this place exists. When the market shuts, and the shops and offices, this is like no-man's land. Back of beyond. You wouldn't think you're in the middle of town – you could have a rave here and nobody would know. See what I mean?'

I looked round the yard. I could see what Naz meant. If you looked at that old wooden door in the wall, you'd never think it opened into a big yard. And apart from that iron gate, it was all solid brick walls around. You'd be on your own here all right.

Naz got up and poured more vodka into my cup.

'It's exclusive, see? Might have been a goods yard once, but now it's our very own club!'

He laughed, and Hami and Bez joined in. I glanced at Joanne and saw she was grinning away too.

It would be like a club, I thought. A grungy club. Cool.

Naz was speaking again. 'Well, what d'you think, Emma. Fancy joining us?'

I looked at Joanne. She was just taking a drag on her fag. As she blew the smoke out, she said, 'Bit different from mall, in't it?'

Joanne was having a dig at me, I was sure. Taking the mick about me being snobby. Well, I wasn't snobby. I'd try anything.

I looked back at Naz. 'Yeah, I'd like to, thanks. Do I have to do owt to join?'

Naz laughed again. 'Just turn up, as and when. That's all.' Then his smile disappeared and he looked serious. 'There is one thing, though, Emma.'

Uh-oh, I thought, what's coming?

'There's just a bunch of us use this place. We don't want everyone knowing about it. I mean it, Emma. If word gets round, all sorts'll turn up and ruin it. You mustn't tell anybody. It's our secret. Can we trust you?'

He was leaning forward and gazing right into my eyes.

''Course you can!' I said. The words practically burst out of me. To tell the truth, I was right flattered that he was trusting me.

I looked over at Joanne. She lifted her paper cup and said, 'Cheers!'

We had a lift back in Hami's car. It wasn't as big and flash as Ali's, but still very comfy inside. I was feeling a sort of happy glow. Not just the booze – we'd had a right good time. A good chat. Couldn't remember what about, exactly, but it was all friendly.

As me and Joanne set off up the road from the village, staggering a bit, I was feeling the effort, so I said, 'Why don't they drive us all the way home?'

Joanne shot me a look.

'D'you really want some nosy parker seeing you? Can't do owt on that estate without someone seeing you and letting on. D'you want your mum and dad to know you've been out boozing with men in town?'

No I didn't, that was for sure. They'd go mental.

'Well, then,' Joanne said, and we fell quiet.

I left her at her gate and walked on to my house. Yeah, good job they did drop us off in the village. This time of night, about half eight, folk were still around, even if most of them were shut indoors watching telly. You never knew if someone might be looking out.

I flopped into bed, feeling fair worn out. But happy, though. Before I drifted off, I found myself thinking it was funny I'd joined a club. I'd never seen the point of being in a gang, doing the same thing at the same time. But this was different, this wasn't a kids' game. This was grown-up. Yeah, it was grown-up.

I smiled to myself at the thought. I belonged to a club, and I liked it.

Another thought just flicked into my head. What would Naz have done if I'd said, 'Nah. I can't keep a secret. I'm gonna tell everybody'? Didn't occur to me at the time. But of course there was no chance of that. He must have known he could trust me.

And that was true. He could depend on me not to say a word. Except to my mates, of course. He couldn't expect me not to let them in on it, and I knew they wouldn't talk out of turn.

Joanne arranged the next meeting at our usual place on a Saturday, the mall. Chloe was better by now, so she met up with the rest of us, me, Joanne and Sophie. We hadn't asked Claire. After what she said the other day, I for one felt a bit cool towards her. Still, we'd manage without her right enough.

While we were waiting for the bus, I filled Chloe in on my adventures that week. She was wide-eyed, took it all in. 'Wish I'd been there,' she said. And I could say, 'You will be.'

At the mall, we were sat in McDonald's as usual, when Joanne suddenly sat up straight in her chair and waved. 'Hiya!'

I looked round and my heart gave a bit of a jump. There was Ali, together with Naz, strolling towards us, big smiles on their faces. Two good-looking guys, smartly turned out, immaculate. Joanne did the introductions, everybody said hi, and the guys pulled a couple of chairs up to our table.

After a bit of chit-chat, Ali said, 'Right, what shall we do this beautiful afternoon?'

And it was a nice day, I remember. A proper autumn day, with golden sunshine.

Ali answered his own question. 'Let's go for a walk,' he said. 'Too nice a day to stay indoors.'

Suits me, I thought. Everyone seemed to agree, and got up. We made our way down the escalator, out the main doors, and turned left to walk along the nearest path through the gardens. First off, there were quite a few folk milling about, by the doors and the concourse, but as we walked along, they seemed to drop off. By the time we reached a big clump of trees, we were the only people around.

'This'll do,' said Joanne, and she walked under the trees towards a couple of seats. She sat with Ali and Naz while I sat with Chloe and Sophie.

For a moment. nobody spoke. We just sort of looked at each other, and at the sky, the ground, birds pecking at stuff...then Ali broke the silence.

'This is nice,' he said, with one of his perfect smiles. The sort of smile that makes you want to smile back, even if you don't know why. 'But I think we could make it nicer.'

He opened his bag, which was like a baggy black briefcase, and real leather, I could tell. He got out a bottle with a familiar label.

'Oh good,' said Chloe. 'I like that one.'

I looked at her in surprise. First I'd heard that she liked vodka at all, let alone having a favourite kind.

Still smiling, Ali unscrewed the top, and passed the bottle to Joanne. As she tipped it back and had a glug, I thought, We're all drinking from the same bottle! Yuk. Then I caught myself. Don't be such a wimp, everyone else's doing it.

Joanne passed the bottle to me, I had a glug and passed it to Chloe, who took two glugs, then it was to Sophie. She was giggling, a bit nervous, I thought, and had a sip. Then it was the guys' turn. They each took a long leisurely pull at the bottle, and Ali stretched his legs out. 'This is the life,' he said. 'Lovely place, lovely girls...'

'I could do with a fag,' said Joanne.

Naz was up in an instant, offering his own little flat box to her, and flicking his lighter. 'Anyone else?' he asked.

A minute later we were all sat there, puffing away, passing the bottle.

As usual, I could feel the drink working its magic, making me feel warm and comfortable. Sophie was relaxing now, and laughed at anything anybody said.

After a while, Naz pulled a package wrapped in paper out of his jacket pocket. He unrolled the paper, and said, 'Anyone want some?'

Spliffs. I recognised them, they looked like big fags, only not so neatly rolled. I'd seen them around, at school, but I'd never tried one. I'd had it drilled into me about drugs, just say no, and so on and on. But I knew for a fact that a lot of kids at our school smoked cannabis, and it didn't seem to do them any harm. It wasn't as if it was hard drugs, like heroin. What worried me was that I might do it wrong, choke and cough and embarrass myself.

Joanne started things off, lighting the spliff with Naz's lighter. She sat there drawing it in. Breathe in, hold it, let it out slowly. Right. That's how Chloe did it, then Sophie. I copied them, tried to look as if I knew what I was doing. Fine. I lost count how many times we lit up, but it must have been the last spliff going round when Sophie did what I'd been afraid of. The smoke got her the wrong way, and she coughed and coughed while Joanne hit her on the back.

I'm sorry to say I thought this was funny. I caught Chloe's eye, and her mouth twitched, and before I knew it, we were laughing as if we could never stop. We set Joanne off, and the three of us fell in a heap on the ground, shaking. We were just about helpless. Though my eyes were streaming, I caught a sight of Ali and Naz, sitting back on the bench, relaxed. I saw them look at each other, and smile. Not a wide smile, a small one.

Sophie was parched, so she needed more vodka. We all finished the bottle, us girls sitting on the ground, Ali and Naz still on the bench.

My head was a whirl. I don't think I'd ever felt so alive, so happy, as if my heart would burst. I looked at my friends, my old friends from school, and loved them to bits. I looked at my new friends, and loved them to bits. I was full of love, and the world was wonderful. Life couldn't get much better than this, that's for sure.

I didn't want to go home. I wanted to stay here, I wanted this afternoon to go on and on. Everywhere else was dull and boring.

'You must get the bus, Emma,' Ali said. He wasn't

smiling, he looked quite serious. 'You must get the bus or you'll be late home, and we don't want that, do we?'

Don't we? I do.

'Gimme a lift,' I said at one time. I think I even said, 'Beemer.' God, how embarrassing. Only it wasn't, somehow. Everyone was mates, you could say what you liked and nobody would mind. Odd bits of memory. I do remember Ali saying quite loudly, 'I don't have the car today.' No beemer. Bummer.

I'm not sure how I got to the bus stop. I think Ali practically carried me. And it wasn't just me who was woozy. Chloe was practically out for the count, and it took Naz and Joanne together to get her moving.

What a laugh. What a huge wonderful laugh. My mood lasted all the way home. I'd never enjoyed a bus ride so much. Never knew it could be so fascinating. I loved that bus...

That was the beginning. The real beginning, I mean, when my world expanded like my mind. I'd thought my life was fine, my ordinary everyday life, but what did I know? From now on, I lived for those times we'd all get together, have a drink, a smoke, a few spliffs. And laughs, always laughs. I kept going to the mall on Saturdays as usual, and started going to town with

Joanne and Chloe at least three times a week, four if we could make it. Fridays were out for me, as I still had to work in the shop in the evening. I knew I still had to keep my head down, look and act as normal, at home and at school. It used to make me giggle sometimes, to think what Mum and Dad didn't know. The secret was part of the fun.

I'd realised after a few sessions and a few hang-overs (which I had to disguise as a bad headache) that I had my limits with drink and dope. I might have enjoyed that first time, when I was off my head, but deep inside I knew that wasn't for me. I had to keep control, had to keep a balance. I worked out pretty quickly that a few glugs of vodka and a couple of spliffs were enough to get me in the mood and keep me there. Chloe, now, grabbed at everything going and got wasted most of the time. She usually ended up being sick, which wasn't very nice. No way would I go down that road. I don't know how we got her home sometimes. Her sister Laura must have covered for her a fair bit. She was older than us, about our Stevie's age. Chloe had told me Laura was into dope, so she was probably used to it.

Us girls were meeting more lads now. I say lads, but they tended to be a bit older, like Ali. Looking back, it was like all these Asian families were connected, and there'd be brothers, and cousins, lots of cousins. Ordinary mates too, of course. I loved the way it went, everybody linked up, like we were one big family. Through Ali and Naz we met some really interesting guys, especially one called Vin. He was into music, and one afternoon at the mall he gave me a listen on his Walkman (these were the days before everyone had iPods). I liked the music straight away. It was edgy, and jumpy, with a strong beat that hooked me.

'What's this called?' I asked Vin.

When he answered, at first I thought he was using a Pakistani word – neesh. When I looked blank, he spelled it out.

'N-I-C-H-E. Niche. Called after this nightclub in Sheffield. Heavy stuff.'

I learned later that this club had a bad reputation for gangs, drugs and shootings. It was shut down later on. But for now, this new music was just another reason to hang out with a great bunch of guys. I could hear stuff I'd never normally be in touch with.

I still wasn't looking at them in a boyfriend kind of way. We didn't kiss or hold hands or anything like that. I knew I didn't feel that way. Maybe I would later, but I wasn't in a hurry. My heart might lift when I saw Ali, but that was more because I admired him and his glamorous lifestyle so much. Chloe didn't go out of her way to attract boys – not that she needed to. She was so beautiful that they were always attracted. Poor Joanne did get crushes on lads, but never got anywhere. I think she was a bit jealous of me and Chloe. Me because I wasn't bothered, really I wasn't, and Chloe because she got a lot of attention and took no notice. It was hard for Joanne. She just didn't have the looks that guys went for straight off. She'd do anything to grab a lad's attention, as me and Chloe would find out soon enough. Before then, though, I'd have my own taste of attention – and I didn't like it.

7
Danger Signs

This particular Saturday, it was just me and Chloe. We were sitting outside the main doors of the mall – the last week of October, and it was still warm enough to sit out in the sun. We'd said hi to a dozen or so lads we knew, as they went into the mall. Then a couple of guys we didn't know were standing in front of us. One of them was a good-looking lad, well dressed, dead smart.

'You're Emma, aren't you?' he asked.

'Yeah,' I said. 'How d'you know?'

'I'm a friend of Vin's,' he said. 'My name's Aman, and this is Ranav.' He waved a hand at his friend, and they both sat down, either side of us.

Ranav was sitting next to Chloe, looking closely at her, and I must say I felt sorry for her. I'd hardly ever seen such an ugly bloke as this Ranav. He was older, much older than Aman, at least thirty I would've said, and his face was enough to put you off your dinner. He had a scar running right down one side of it, which twisted his mouth. His eyes were small and mean-looking, and his skin wasn't nice and smooth – it was all pitted and rough. And he had a funny sort of beard, thin lines going down in front of his ears and meeting under his chin, joining up with a thin moustache. It made him look sinister, like a villain in the films. He was perfectly well dressed, but no amount of classy clothes would make him good-looking.

Aman was speaking again. 'Fancy going for a walk?'

What? That was a bit sudden.

I shook my head. 'No, I'm all right, thanks. I'll stay with Chloe.'

I could tell from the look on her face that she didn't want to be left alone with the ugly one.

'Oh go on,' Aman said. 'Let's take a walk in the gardens.'

He did look nice, and I didn't want to seem unfriendly, or even rude. That's not how you make new friends, is it?

'Let's all go,' I said, and we stood up together. Chloe kept by my side as we walked along. Very pleasant, chatting away about this and that. Then, I don't know how it happened, I was walking one way with Aman, and Chloe was walking another way with Ranav. Me and Aman were standing under a tree, and he was leaning into me, pressing my body with his.

'I'd like to know you better, Emma,' he said, his mouth right close to my face. And next thing his hands were all over my body, touching me up, and he was trying to put his hand down the front of my jeans.

Bloody nerve! I pushed him away.

'Gerroff,' I said, very sharp. 'Gerroff me. I'm going back.' And I marched off towards the main doors.

'You come back here, Emma!' Aman shouted, fierce-like.

You prat, I thought. Out loud I called out, 'No. Leave off.'

I was keeping an eye out for Chloe, and I saw her near the doors.

'Come on,' I said, 'let's go. That Aman tried to touch me up, the prat.'

Chloe grinned. 'Ranav tried it on with me too – no chance, ugly bastard. He in't touching my hand, let alone owt else he had on his mind.'

We decided to have an ice cream before we left, and headed for the Italian place. It was while we were eating our ice creams on a first-floor balcony that we caught sight of the two guys again.

'Look,' said Chloe, pointing downwards with her spoon. 'Didn't take Aman long to get over you, did it?'

I looked down, and sure enough there he was, all smiles, talking to a girl about my age.

'Not broken-hearted, then,' I said, and we laughed.

We saw Ranav too, standing to one side of his mate, looking a bit awkward, shifting on his feet.

'You know what,' Chloe said. 'I reckon Ranav hangs out with Aman cos he's too ugly to get a look in with girls all by himself. Aman chats 'em up, then Ranav grabs what's going.'

We laughed a lot, so I can't say we were traumatised by the experience. I was shocked, sure enough – it was the first time anyone had tried it on with me. And I was angry at Aman taking such a liberty without so much as a by your leave. When I got close to a boy, it wouldn't be like that. I'd have to fancy him first, I knew that.

There was something at the back of my mind, though, and on the bus home I mentioned it to Chloe.

'I suppose…it's nice for a lad to fancy you. Sort of…flattering, like.'

'Only if he's good-looking,' Chloe shot back, and we laughed again.

But I did feel sort of flattered. I might have fancied boys before, from a distance, but I hadn't really thought of it the other way round, them fancying me, and acting on it. A new thought, one I didn't know what to do with.

It never occurred to me that Aman, and Ranav too, come to that, might have had something else in mind. Trying it on with us, that's for sure, but more than that – trying us out.

First chance I had, I told Joanne what had happened. I don't know what I was expecting her to say, but she just shrugged.

'Don't you think it's out of order?' I asked her.

'Well,' she said, with a frown on her face. 'They've not tried owt with me. Maybe you and Chloe led 'em on.'

That made me catch my breath.

'What? What's that you're saying, Joanne? No way did we lead 'em on.'

I must have looked right angry, not like me at all. Joanne glanced at me and started to back down.

'Oh, take no notice. I don't mean it. I'm out of sorts, is all.'

I still glared at her, hands on my hips. I was thinking, Friend or no friend, nobody says something like that about me and gets away with it.

Joanne said, 'Look, Emma. I'm sorry, okay? And sorry if you and Chloe were upset.'

Now it was my turn to shrug.

'Oh, didn't bother us, not really. Just a bit surprised. And it were a bloody nerve all right.'

'Yeah,' she said. She looked so down, I thought I'd drop it. Maybe she was telling the truth. She was low, and just taking it out on me.

Still, I told Chloe what Joanne had said, when I met her at the bus stop in the village after school. We were on our way to town. It was nothing special that we weren't with Joanne. I wasn't blanking her or anything. I'd got over what she said. It was just that sometimes she was off out somewhere without telling us where. Maybe we'd meet up with her later, maybe we wouldn't. And to tell the truth, Chloe was a lot easier to get on with than Joanne. Joanne could be dead moody, but Chloe was a ray of sunshine most of the time. Even when she overdid it and fell over, off her head, she didn't moan. And she always seemed to bounce back with a grin on her face.

Anyway, when I told her what Joanne had said, she just said, 'Huh. Bet I know why.'

I had to ask her. 'Why?'

'She's dead jealous, that lass. If she said the guys hadn't tried it on with her, maybe she wanted them to. She's pissed off with them, and pissed off with us.'

I thought this over. Yeah, it made sense, Joanne wanting to pull boys and them not playing.

Chloe said, 'And you know what? She's got her eye on Kaz, that's for sure. And I reckon he's got his eye on you. If I've seen it, bet Joanne has. Make her even more mardy.'

'Kaz?' I said. 'Don't be daft.'

Chloe just shrugged and grinned. 'Suit yourself,' she said.

In the bus, I thought about what Chloe had said, about Kaz. We hadn't known him long. We'd met him in the club, as I thought of it. He was a friend of someone there. We always met someone new through someone else we already knew. Early twenties, quite good-looking, though nothing special, a bit pushy. Almost the first thing he said to me was a compliment. 'Beautiful blue eyes,' he'd said, big smile on his face, tracing his finger down my cheek. I just moved my head back. That was so corny. Sometimes the guys paid compliments, but it wasn't mushy. Just part of being friendly.

There was another thing about Kaz, something that bothered me. Though I didn't know much about the lives of these guys, outside when we met them, I did hear odd bits of stuff. Before Kaz even spoke to me, I'd heard him complaining.

'Never bloody stops,' he said. 'Doing my head in.'

I gathered he had a new baby, who was crying a lot. Did that mean he was married? That gave me a bit of a shock. I hadn't thought of these guys as having families. Well, mums and dads, I suppose, and brothers and sisters, but not being married with kids. The way I'd been brought up, if a man had kids, he looked out for them, didn't go around moaning about them. I thought back to my dad. We might not be getting on too well now – he was always going on at me about homework and stuff, and being out at weekends – but I'd never forget what he did for me and Stevie when we were little. I was feeling sorry for Kaz's wife, when he came up to me all smarmy.

No, I didn't fancy him one bit. If Joanne liked him, she was welcome to him. Though he hadn't shown much sign of fancying her. A couple of times I'd heard him being downright rude to her, and shrugging her hand off if she touched his arm. 'Get off, yer big lump,' he'd snapped at her. Charming. Joanne had looked upset.

This night, I wondered if he'd be around. We didn't always go to the club. Over the past few weeks, we'd wandered round town quite a bit, hanging out. There was another place we all liked, a few streets away from the market. It was an old war memorial, one of those big stone pillars with lots of names carved into it, and poppies left there once a year. Behind this was a little square of garden, with grass and bushes and benches. It was fenced off, and the gate was locked in the evening, but we just climbed over, no sweat. It was quiet and peaceful. Nobody bothered us there.

This evening was a bit chilly, which showed winter was coming. It'd been a lovely October, but now we were having to wear coats and jackets. Tonight I was wearing a coat over my jacket, it was that parky.

'Which way?' I said to Chloe when we got off the bus.

'Um...' Then she nodded. 'War memorial.'

Fine by me. One of the things I liked about hanging out was that you never knew who was going to be there. If it was someone you liked, so much the better.

As we walked up to the memorial, we could see half a dozen guys lounging about. Not many other folk were around, now the market had shut and the shops and offices too. As we got nearer, Chloe nudged me. 'You're in luck,' she said, grinning. 'Lover boy's here.'

Sure enough, there was Kaz.

'Don't take the piss,' I muttered to her.

Then it was 'Hiya, girls' from the guys, and smiles all round.

As we climbed over the gate, I noticed someone else sat on one of the old wooden benches, huddled up. Joanne! I hadn't seen her, hidden behind the guys. She looked up as me and Chloe arrived. She didn't smile at us, just nodded, and looked away. Something was bothering her, that was sure. Maybe we'd talk later on. Meanwhile, me and Chloe settled ourselves down on another bench, and were soon smoking fags and swigging out the bottle of vodka someone offered us. A spliff or two and everything was rosy.

Then Kaz plonked himself next to me.

'Hi, beautiful,' he said to me. What a prat. What did he think he was after? And though I might be getting mellow, it didn't mean I looked on him any more kindly. I still thought it was out of order, him chatting up girls when he was married. I didn't know much about Muslim customs then, but I was sure two-timing your wife wouldn't be approved of.

In the time I'd known these Asian guys, I'd picked up a bit about their religion. Muslims were against booze and pork. Well, I'd never seen a guy eating a bacon sandwich, but the booze ban didn't seem to be working! I knew a few of them went to what they called their mosque on Fridays, like a church, but what that meant I'd no idea.

Now Kaz was saying, 'Let's go for a walk, Emma.'

'I'm all right, thanks,' I said. Something about him made me shiver, and he said, 'Look, you're cold. A walk'll warm you up. Come on.'

And he held me by my elbow. What should I do? I didn't want to walk anywhere with him, that was for sure, but I didn't want to seem rude. It wasn't as if he was being rude himself, he was perfectly polite. Maybe I'd just go for a quick turn round the block and that'd get him off my back.

'Okay,' I said.

He grinned, and said, 'Let's go down alley.'

Yeah, I thought. That's a nice place for a walk. This alley was behind the war memorial gardens, but you could get into it through a broken bit of fence at the back. It was just a path between buildings, old factories, I think, and going nowhere in particular. Still, I strolled off, hands in pockets. I really was getting chilly. Not for the first time, I wished we had a place indoors we could meet. We did hang out in cars sometimes, so I hoped we'd be doing more of that in winter.

Kaz walked close beside me, holding the broken bits of plank apart so I could dodge through. When we'd walked up the alley a bit, he suddenly grabbed me and pulled me towards him. At the same time he was unzipping my coat, and before I could do anything he'd unzipped my jacket too.

Bloody hell, I thought. He's trying it on, just like Aman. I pushed myself away from him, and wrapped my coat round me.

'Leave off,' I said, sharp as I could.

I could see Kaz's face in the light of a street lamp the other side of the end wall. He didn't look angry, more upset.

'Look,' he said. 'I didn't mean owt. I were just being friendly.'

Yeah, right. Well, you can be friendly from over there, I thought.

He just stood there, awkward like, blinking a lot, staring at me. Suddenly I felt a bit sorry for him. I had to put him off, but I didn't want to be nasty. Then I had a brainwave. At least, I thought it was a brainwave.

'Look, Kaz,' I said. 'It's not I don't like you or owt. But Joanne really likes you, you know she does. What would she think if she knew I let you try it on with me?' I shook my head. 'You can't do that to a mate.'

Kaz was scowling, his hands jammed into his jacket pockets. I turned round to go back but he grabbed my arm and said, 'Wait a minute.'

'What?'

He muttered something and I couldn't catch it.

'What?' I said again.

'Go and get Joanne, then,' he said through his teeth.

Right, that'll cheer her up, I thought.

'Okay.' And I walked quickly off. As I went back through the fence, I could see the others where I'd left them. There were clouds of smoke drifting round them, very sweet. Joanne was looking straight at me, frowning. I'd finished zipping up my jacket and coat by the time I reached her, and said, 'Joanne, Kaz's asking for you.'

Her face brightened. 'Is he?' she asked, getting to her feet. She practically ran through the garden to the fence. I just thought, No accounting for tastes, and sat back next to Chloe.

Another couple of swigs and I was warming up again. I kept an eye on my watch. We mustn't miss our bus back to the village. I wondered if Joanne would be coming back with us.

I'm not sure how much time passed, it was that pleasant, till Chloe said, 'Joanne's taking a time. Wonder what she's doing.'

'Well, she's still down alley,' I said. I might be getting mellow, but I think I would've noticed if she'd walked past.

Chloe stood up. 'I'm gonna go and see what's keeping her,' she announced.

'I'll come with you,' I said, and got up too.

We got through the broken fence, and strolled up the alley. Towards the end we could see a shape. I couldn't make it out at first, then as we got closer I realised it was Kaz standing up, and Joanne on her knees in front of him. Her head was buried in his crotch, moving just a bit.

'Oh my God,' muttered Chloe. 'She's only giving him a blow job! Let's get outta here.' And we scurried back to where we'd been sat, not saying another word.

With the guys around, we couldn't talk about what we'd seen. We just drew on our fags, and listened to the chat going on around us. I wondered if Chloe was as shocked as me. Though I wasn't sure why I was shocked. I'd heard of blow jobs, of course, but I was a virgin, very much so, and I believe Chloe was too. No way could I imagine myself ever doing that to a guy. It's not that I thought it was especially disgusting or anything. Everything about sex was a bit of a mystery. Then again, if it was a guy I liked very much…maybe it'd be different. Yeah, I thought, that's what's bothering me. Kaz doesn't like Joanne, that was obvious. She must know, so how could she do that? What was she thinking?

Then I felt a pang. It was me who told her to go and see him, passed on the message. What was I thinking? Not blow jobs, that's for sure. If I thought about anything, I thought maybe he'd chat her up, have a kiss. Try it on, feel her up...oh, I don't know. Anyway, Joanne's a big girl, she's knows more than me, she can take care of herself.

My thoughts were going round and round till suddenly Joanne was standing there in front of us. As me and Chloe looked up, she said, 'I'm off to get bus. Coming?' And she turned on her heel and marched off. Me and Chloe hurried after her, just saying 'Bye!' to the guys.

When we caught up with her, Joanne said, 'Don't say owt.'

'But—' I started, and Joanne said, more sharp, 'I said, don't say owt.'

In the light of the street lamps I could see her face was flushed, and her eyes were bright, as if there were tears there. We walked to the bus stop in silence. The streets were so quiet you could hear the tap-tap of our boot heels. The bus was on time, and Joanne sat by herself, looking out the window. She was biting her lower lip.

When we got off, we said goodnight to Chloe, and she was off home. Joanne marched up our road very fast. I had to practically run to keep up. When she got to her gate, I said, 'See you tomorrow.'

She stopped and looked at me. 'Yeah,' she said. 'See you tomorrow.'

Well, me and Chloe weren't going to let it rest. We had to say something, and next day at school in the dinner hour we went up to Joanne and said, 'We gotta talk.'

One each side of Joanne, we walked over to a quiet place in the playground, and sat down. No one said anything for a moment, Joanne just staring into space. Then Chloe burst out, 'Joanne! How could you! How could you do that!'

'What d'you mean?' said Joanne, her face going red. She folded her arms, and looked bolshie.

'You know what I mean,' Chloe went on. 'How could you do that with him?'

Joanne sat up straight. 'Don't know what you mean,' she said, loud.

'Yeah you do,' Chloe said. Then she spoke softer and added, 'We saw you.'

'Oh.' Joanne seemed to sink into herself. Then she turned to me.

'Well, what about you, Emma? What were you getting up to back there? I saw you, coming out doing up your zips. You'd had them clothes off, you had.'

'What?' I couldn't believe how wrong Joanne was. 'Kaz unzipped them but I didn't take them off, no way. I didn't want owt to do with him.'

'Yeah you did,' she shot back. 'You fancy him. You know I like him and you were getting in there, you cow!'

This was too much. 'Joanne, you've got it all wrong,' I said, gripping her arm. 'No way do I fancy him. I know you like him, and that's what I said to him when he tried it on. "Joanne likes you," I said. "I couldn't go behind a mate's back." That's when he told me to go and get you.'

'Oh,' Joanne said again, and she sat back against the seat. Then she said, 'But that's what he said to me. He said you'd give him a blow job cos that'd make him like you.'

I looked at her. 'Oh, Joanne,' I said. 'That's so not true. I never did. It's you falling for it.'

'Yeah,' Chloe chimed in. 'He's using you, Joanne. He don't like you. I've heard him – he's that horrible to you.'

'That's not true!' Joanne flared back. 'He does like me, he does.'

We were all quiet, then Chloe said, 'Joanne, what makes you think he likes you?'

There were tears tipping out of Joanne's eyes now. 'He in't rough,' said Joanne. 'He strokes my hair.'

Me and Chloe looked at each other. What could you say?

8

Just Doing a Mate a Favour

I felt that sorry for Joanne, being taken in. Big tough Joanne, doing what a guy wants because she wants him to like her. Though I didn't know a lot about stuff, didn't know much about relationships at all, I knew that would never work. He was just taking advantage.

It was because I felt sorry for Joanne that I said yes when she asked me to go to town with her the next time she asked. That day, the first Monday in November, wasn't supposed to be about Joanne and her problems. As far as me and my family were concerned, it was the day Stevie left home for the first time. He'd had notice from the company, and he was off up north for what he called induction. We were seeing him off at Leeds station. I had the day off school as it was a special occasion. Dad had arranged someone to help Joanie in the shop till he and Mum got back.

It was all a bit tense at home that morning. Mum was looking upset, though trying to put a brave face on it. Dad looked choked too. He fussed and flapped round Stevie, saying, 'Have you got this? Have you got that?' till Stevie said straight out, 'I'm all right, Dad. Leave off.' When he's anxious, Dad does tend to flap. I suppose it is emotional when your child leaves home. I knew I was going to miss Stevie, but I tried to be cheerful. Didn't want him going off leaving a lot of long faces behind. He was dead excited, really looking forward to it. He was chatting away in the car as Dad drove us all to the station about midday.

We got there with forty minutes to spare. Dad had been worried there'd be road blocks or something and Stevie would miss his train. So there was plenty of time to have a coffee on the platform.

'Sure you don't want owt to eat, Stevie?' Mum said.

He just laughed. 'What, as well as what you've packed for me?'

Mum was already worrying about Stevie looking after himself, eating the right things. He was on the chubby side already, a right one for his chips and butties, not to mention the ale he'd got a taste for. 'Don't fret, Nicky,' said Dad. (And he was one to talk!) 'He'll be working that hard, weight'll drop off him.'

The clock ticked round, then we heard the train announced and Stevie was gathering up his bags. Mum hugged him and kissed him again and again. Dad shook his hand, then flung his arms round him. 'Take care, son,' he said, and I felt tears coming to my eyes too. Stevie hugged and kissed me. 'Look after yourself, young Emma,' he said.

Then the train was in, engine rattling and banging as loud as you like, and folk were hurrying about as doors opened and shut. Then the train was off. We kept waving till the train went round a corner, when Stevie couldn't have seen us even if he'd looked out a window. Now Mum was weepy, clutching Dad's arm. He put his arms round both of us, and said, 'He'll be fine. He'll be fine. Don't you worry.'

It was early afternoon by the time we got back home. Mum had a meat pie waiting in the fridge and she heated it up for our dinner. All of us just picked at it, even Dad, who's usually got a good appetite.

Then Mum and Dad got ready to go to the shop.

'You'll be all right, love?' asked Mum.

''Course I will,' I said, though to tell the truth, I felt right tired. Didn't know why – I hadn't been doing much all day. 'I'll catch up with me homework, then I'll probably go round Chloe's when she's back from school.'

'Right you are,' said Mum, and she and Dad drove off. The house seemed very quiet. I wasn't usually in all by myself at this time of day. It was funny to think we wouldn't be hearing Stevie clunking about, saying, 'Where's me socks?' or whatever. Me and Mum were always going on at him for dropping his stuff all over the place. It'd be strange for a room to stay exactly as tidy as it was.

I just flopped in the living room. Maybe watch a bit of telly. I was dozing off when the phone rang, waking me up sharpish.

It was Joanne.

'Oh, Emma – good, you're back. How'd it go, with your Stevie?'

'Okay,' I said.

'Well, it's like this. Could you do us a favour? I've had me mobile pinched and I'm gonna go to police station in town. Don't fancy going by meself.'

This didn't sound like Joanne, I thought. She was never backward coming forward. Then again, hadn't I seen she wasn't as tough as she seemed? To be honest, I felt a bit whacked, but I thought it'd be a good chance to get back in with Joanne, get back to our old friendship. What are mates for?

'Okay,' I said. Then I remembered I was going to meet Chloe.

'Hang on,' I said. 'I've gotta ring Chloe, let her know.'

'Fine,' said Joanne. 'See if she'll come too.'

'Right. I'll come down now, shall I?'

'Yeah, thanks. I'll be at gate.'

Before I left I phoned Chloe. She'd been back from school for a while, and was happy to come out. So me and Joanne met her in the village. On the bus, Joanne filled us in.

'I were in town yesterday with Mary.' (Mary was an older girl Joanne was friends with – I didn't really know her.) 'Well, we met up with some guys, some Asian guys, and one of them asked if he could borrow my mobile for a bit – he'd lost his and there were a call he were wanting to make. If I'd thought, I'd have said, "Why don't you borrow one off your mate?" But no, like an idiot I lent him mine, and he only went and buggered off with it. I know who he is and I'm gonna tell police.'

And that's the story she told to the policeman behind the desk at the station. Me and Chloe hung back a bit while Joanne told him about it. 'And I know his name,' she finished off.

The policeman, an old fat guy with grey hair, looked at her and said, 'You know his name, love? That'll make our job easier, won't it?'

'It's Tarik,' Joanne said.

'Tarik?' the policeman said. 'Is that his first name or his surname?'

Joanne shrugged. 'I dunno,' she said. 'It's just what he's called.'

The policeman was shaking his head. 'Well, love, I don't know how many Tariks there are round about here, first name or second name. Reckon we need a bit more to go on. Can you find out his full name?'

'I dunno,' said Joanne again. 'S'pose I can have a go.'

'You do that, love,' said the policeman, 'and we'll see what we can do.'

He didn't seem that bothered, to tell the truth. Folk must get their mobiles pinched all the time. And it's not as if anybody was hurt. Joanne stomped off out of the station, me and Chloe following.

'Fat lot of good that was,' said Joanne.

'Would you know this bloke if you saw him again?' asked Chloe. 'The one who nicked your phone, I mean.'

'Oh, I'd know him all right,' said Joanne.

'Well, maybe if you see him again, you could ask someone what his name is?'

'Yeah,' said Joanne. The fight seemed to have gone out of her. 'I'm starving – fancy a McDonald's? My treat.'

The McDonald's was on the way back to the bus stop, so we piled in and had our usual burgers and chips.

I was wondering whether we'd go on to the club, or hang around the war memorial, or whether Joanne wasn't in the mood. Turned out she was in the mood for socialising. 'Now we're here,' she said. So we thought we'd try the memorial, see who was around. And the odd drink or spliff would help me lighten up. I was a bit down, I realised, now that Stevie had gone. Though I didn't know then just what a help a big brother could have been to me.

There was a bunch of guys hanging around the garden behind the memorial, we saw as we got nearer. Some of them saw us and waved us over. I had a quick look round to see if Kaz was there. He wasn't, I'm glad to say.

Some guys were making room on benches for us to sit down when Joanne suddenly stood stock still. Then she pointed at a guy, who was sat casual like on the arm of a bench, smoking a fag.

'You!' she said loudly. 'You! Of all the bloody nerve! How you've got the brass face to sit there and—'

'And what, Joanne?'

The guy she was talking to didn't move, except to put the fag in his mouth again. He was smiling a small smile all the time. His voice wasn't loud, like Joanne's, but it somehow got through to you, as if it was cutting its way. I had a good look at him in the light of the street lamp.

He was Kaz's age, I thought, early twenties, quite slightly built. Thick dark hair slicked back from a wide forehead. Large eyes, straight nose, strongly shaped mouth. He had one of those thin beards, like Ranav had, only on this guy it looked good, sharp. He was smartly dressed all in black, or at least what looked black in this light. Top coat, over a suit, shirt undone at the neck. He was relaxed as he leant against the wall, lifting an eyebrow at Joanne as he blew smoke lazily out of his mouth.

I found myself staring at him. To tell the truth, I couldn't take my eyes off him. What was it? There he was, quiet, not doing anything, except taking the mick out of Joanne, yet I felt something…a prickling at the back of my neck, my stomach sort of going tight. I wish I could say that I was picking up evil vibes coming off him. But I can't. Nothing like that entered my head. I was just fascinated by him, right from the off, and I didn't know why.

Now Joanne was spluttering with anger. 'You bastard, you nicked my phone. It were only a lend, I didn't give it you, and I want it back, understand?'

So this was the guy who nicked her phone? Tarik, she'd called him.

He shook his head, side to side, slowly.

'Joanne, Joanne,' he said softly, but still you could hear him. 'What are you saying? How could you think I'd nick anything from you?'

'Cos you bloody well did!'

Tarik's eyebrows rose. 'I'm shocked, Joanne. Shocked. There was me thinking you'd given it to me out of the kindness of your heart. I needed to make a call and didn't have one, and you gave me one. Gave me, not lent. I said thank you, and thought you were very kind.' He shrugged. 'Now look at you!'

And Joanne was a bit of a sight, standing rigid with her shoulders hunched up, her hair every which way, her face twisted. She kept on at him.

'What have you done with it? Where is it?'

Tarik gazed at her, finishing off his fag. He flipped the stub away as he said, 'Sold it.'

Joanne spluttered some more. 'Sold it! Of all the bloody nerve—'

'You're repeating yourself, Joanne,' said Tarik, cutting in. His voice was smooth, but not in a smarmy way. It seemed to vibrate, as if it was a musical instrument. I was fascinated.

All this time, the other guys had been watching

them both, just like me and Chloe. Now one of them, Hassan, moved forward, and said, 'Look, what's a mobile between friends? No point kicking up a shindig in public. Joanne, if you want a mobile I'll get you one, okay? Settle down.'

Tarik's small smile was turning into a wide grin as Hassan spoke. 'Hear that, Joanne?' he said. 'Can't say fairer than that, now, can we?'

Joanne was breathing heavily, but she turned to Hassan and said, 'Yeah, okay. Great.'

Tarik got off the arm of the bench and walked up to Joanne, holding out his hand. 'Friends again?' he said. Joanne glared at him for a moment, then shook his hand quickly before pulling away.

'Good,' said Tarik. Then he turned to look straight at me, then at Chloe. I got the full force of those eyes, and what it was I don't know. They were just eyes, dark eyes, but they seemed to hold you... He was speaking again.

'Joanne, why don't you introduce me to your friends? I don't believe we've met.'

'Chloe and Emma,' Joanne muttered, no frills.

He shook hands with us in turn, very polite. 'Delighted to meet you,' he said to us both. His smile was warm, and I felt myself warmed.

I could have stood there like a lemon, forgetting to

let go of his hand, but Joanne's voice cut in sharp. 'We gotta go, get the bus. Come on.'

'Safe journey home,' said Tarik. He stepped back and waved as Joanne pulled me and Chloe by the arm and hustled us off up the street. We heard a chorus of 'Goodnight' and 'Bye' from the other guys behind us.

None of us said a word on the way to the bus stop. As we stood waiting, I was rerunning the scene with Tarik in my mind. It wasn't till we were sat on the bus that one of us spoke.

'Are you gonna find out Tarik's other name, then?' Chloe asked.

Joanne made a face. 'Dunno.'

'But he nicked your phone,' Chloe went on. 'Didn't he?'

'Yeah,' said Joanne. 'Dunno if I can be arsed now, though.'

'But you were mad enough at him to go to the police,' said Chloe.

Joanne sighed. 'Yeah. But if Hassan's gonna get me a new one...'

Chloe made a noise that sounded like Tcha! and sat back in her seat.

'I just don't get you, Joanne,' she said. 'One minute you're all fired up, next minute you're letting this Tarik get away with it.'

'Well, I were that pissed off at start,' said Joanne. 'But what's the point? You can never get owt past Tarik. He's always got an answer. Dunno why I bothered in first place.'

'Yeah, why did you?' Chloe seemed to be getting upset.

'Summat up?' I asked her, all direct.

She was quiet for a minute, then burst out, 'It's that bloke, that Tarik. He gives me the creeps! Dunno what it is, but I got a bad feeling.'

Joanne shrugged. 'Oh, he's okay,' she said.

'What?' said Chloe. 'He nicked your phone and he's okay?'

'Yeah, well, forget it. In't worth the bother.'

And Joanne looked out of the window for the rest of the ride home.

I sat in my seat, thinking about what Chloe said. So she'd felt something coming from Tarik too, like I did, but it took her a different way. I found him attractive, sort of, but she thought the opposite. I tried to puzzle it out, but by the time I got home I was none the wiser.

It turned out that Chloe was right from the start.

9

Getting to Know Him

I was that proud, I could've burst. Didn't want to show it, of course, so I tried to act casual, walking along the high street next to Tarik as if it was the most ordinary thing in the world.

Tarik. I couldn't believe I'd actually got to know him. I never dreamed he'd want to be my friend. I was friends with a lot of the Asian guys in town, and I'd pretty much taken it for granted. Why shouldn't they want to know me? I was smart, I knew stuff and I liked a laugh. In short, I was good company. But from the off, Tarik seemed out of my league, a cut above the rest. Months ago, I'd thought Ali had had it all – good looks, smart clothes, nice manners – but Tarik put him in the shade. He had all that and more. He was different. I could never work it out, what exactly made him different. It's not as if he made a song and dance about anything, or raised his voice, but people took notice of him, they listened to him. And they respected him.

I could see the respect in people's eyes as we walked along. They'd glance at him, catch his eye, and their own eyes would drop down, just for a second or two, as they gave a quick nod. I realised that people accepted what he said, didn't argue, whatever it was – even if it was something like whether we walked somewhere or drove. There might be a bit of banter, but nobody came straight out and disagreed with him.

Later, I knew what it was that he had: charisma. I wouldn't even have heard the word then, but when I did, and learned what it meant, I knew. That's Tarik, I thought. Something about him, a power, that attracted you, a sort of charm, but not the smarmy sort. It didn't make you feel comfortable, or easy. There was an edge to it, just the slightest hint that there was something that could be off the wall, exciting.

I wondered if Joanne felt it. She'd made a big fuss about him nicking her phone, and later I thought maybe this was her putting on an act, to get his attention. After all, it was obvious that Tarik wasn't short of a few bob, as my dad says when people are well off. Maybe his phone was broken, or something, and he just asked Joanne for a lend for a call he had to make there and then, but she insisted he took it, like a present. That would mean he owed her, give a reason for her to hang out with him. Maybe he was teasing her when he said he sold it. Joanne's moods could get to you, you'd want to make her shut up. Oh, I don't know.

I do know that Chloe never changed her mind about him.

'He's over there – don't look!'

'What?' I said, turning my head straight away.

'I said don't look!' Chloe was practically hissing.

'What?' I said again. 'Who're you talking about?'

'It's him,' she said. 'That Tarik, who nicked Joanne's phone. Oh my God!' Her voice was rising. 'He's coming this way. Don't look.' And she stared at her bottle of Coke as if it was the most important thing in the world.

I didn't look round, though I was tempted. Nah, he was just passing through. Everybody passed through the mall at one time or other if you waited long enough. Why should he come by us? Still, my heart was beating fast, and the back of my neck prickled.

Then I heard his voice, light and deep at the same time.

'Emma! Chloe! How nice to see you again.'

And he was pulling out a chair and sitting at our table. He was only sitting at our table!

I tried to act natural. 'Good to see you too, Tarik,' I said. I thought I'd mention his name straight up, to show I remembered his as he remembered ours.

He leant back in his chair and smiled, easy. 'You girls been shopping?'

Chloe didn't lift her eyes from her Coke. She'd just looked up at him quickly when he arrived, muttered hi and looked back at her drink. It was up to me to be sociable, that was for sure.

'A bit,' I said. 'Nothing special. How about you?'

He shrugged. 'Nothing special,' he said back. 'But that's not the point of this place, is it?' He was smiling straight at me now.

'What?' I said, just as pleasant, trying out a smile. 'A shopping mall in't the place to shop?'

He smiled wider at that. 'You know what I mean,' he said. 'It's where you meet up with your friends, hang out with them. If you buy something, fine, but that's by the way. Don't you think?'

I'd have agreed with anything he said, but I didn't want to look like a puppy, as if I didn't have a mind of my own.

'Well,' I said, 'I like hanging out and I like shopping too. Best of both worlds.'

That actually made him laugh, laugh out loud. 'Lucky girl,' he said. 'You're in the right place then, aren't you?' Then he added, 'What do you think, Chloe?'

She had to look up at him then, but she just shrugged, and said, 'Not bothered, me.'

Tarik didn't seem put out, just smiled again, lifting one eyebrow. Then he said, 'Well, much as I'd like to, I can't sit here all day. You know what they say – places to go, people to see...'

And he got to his feet.

'Hope to see you again soon,' he said. And with a wave of his hand he turned and walked away, heading for the escalator. I watched him till he disappeared. Suddenly I heard Chloe say, 'Best of both worlds!' in a silly, squeaky voice. Right sarky, too.

'What?' I said.

'Oh Emma,' she said in her ordinary voice. 'What are you like? Sucking up to that man like that.'

'I weren't!' I said. 'Just being sociable.' I felt my cheeks burning. I must be going red.

'Yeah, right.'

'What's the matter with you?' I shot back at her.

'What's the matter with me?' she said. 'It's you, Emma. If your tongue was hanging out any more you'd have been licking floor.'

That got to me. 'I don't know what you mean,' I

said. 'He were only here a coupla minutes. Just a bit of banter—'

'Bit of banter my arse,' said Chloe. 'You couldn't take your eyes off him.'

I was gobsmacked. How could she see and hear what happened and talk of it like this? A thought suddenly shot into my mind. Was she jealous of him talking to me? Maybe that was it. Just as quick, I thought, no, she didn't like him from the off.

'Look,' I said. 'What have you got against Tarik? What's he done to you?'

Chloe shook her head. 'He in't done nothing to me. It's just the way he is. He gives me the creeps.'

'You don't even know him,' I said.

'Nor do you,' she said. 'You fancy him, don't you?'

'No I don't!' I said that really loud, and out the corner of my eye I could see heads turning in our direction. I made my voice low, and said again, 'No. It's not that. There's nothing wrong with him.'

Chloe sighed. 'Look, I don't wanna fall out with you or owt, Emma. 'Specially not about him. He's a nasty piece of work, I just know he is. I got a feeling.' Now she was standing up and grabbing her bag. 'But if you see him again, keep an eye out. I gotta go now – see you later.'

And she was off, leaving me at the table holding my

own Coke. I was quite shocked, all round. First off, shocked that Tarik had turned up. That was in a good way. Second, that Chloe had practically attacked me. That was bad – it was all over nothing. What does she know? I thought to myself. Saying I fancy him. I don't.

And that was true. It really wasn't fancying in the way of wanting to get close up and personal with a boy. I know I've said it before, but at this time I really didn't have sexual feelings. I knew that other girls went out with boys and even went all the way, I'd heard it at school. The thought just left me cold. What a lot of fuss, I'd think. Later on, when I grew up, I did recognise sexual feelings, so it's not as if I don't know what they are. What I felt for Tarik at that time was...well, I admired him. He impressed me. I liked his confidence – it was a quiet confidence, which is more impressive than shouting about it. And yes, I must say that seeing that other people admired him built him up in my eyes even more. There was a sort of power there.

I just couldn't see why Chloe didn't like him. A feeling, she says! What's that? That's not anything. She's just taken against him for no reason. Maybe she is jealous after all.

I sat there for a while, pissed off that Chloe had left. We usually went home together on a Saturday and spent a lot of time together the rest of the week. We'd taken to leaving school together, and walking off the road down a little lane to a clump of trees in a field. We'd roll a couple of joints and have a couple of drinks, get mellow for the evening. Magic. A few times, Sophie joined us, but I can't say she was ever as keen as me and Chloe. Good company, though. Talking of old friends, Claire had just about dropped off the radar by now – a shame, as she was always so nice.

Sometimes Joanne would come with us – she was the one who'd usually buy the booze, as she could easily pass for eighteen, she was that developed. Chloe got the dope from her sister Laura. We'd club together, and we never went short. For me, I was still working, or sort of working, in the shop on Fridays, so I had my tenner for that. Then there was five pounds pocket money from Mum and Dad, and Nan often gave me a fiver too. 'Treat yourself, pet,' she'd say. I didn't need telling twice!

A nice set-up. Was Chloe going to give that up? Well, if she didn't want my company, I didn't want hers. Calls herself a mate!

Well, if Chloe didn't want to be with me, there was always Joanne. And I mean that – she was always there. Asked me to come out with her practically every day. During the week, we'd catch the bus to town after school, and hang around where the action was. On Saturdays it was always the mall. What with the weather getting colder, I liked staying in the warm.

It was one Thursday, when me and Joanne were on the bus to town, that she told me we were going somewhere different.

'Mate of Tarik's just got this pub,' she said. 'Red Lion – d'you know it?'

My ears pricked up at the mention of Tarik's name, but as I'd never been much of a one for pubs, I shook my head.

'Well,' she went on, 'there's a room in it, not one of the bars, that we could go in.' She looked over at me and said, 'Well, I mean that you can go in.' I knew what she meant. There was her, looking just about grown up, and there was me, looking about eleven – and I'd be fourteen in six months' time! Not fair.

I liked the idea of being indoors, so instead of making a beeline for the war memorial, or for what I still called the club, we went a different way and arrived at this pub. It looked a bit run-down, to be honest, paint peeling and all, and I said so.

'Oh, Emma,' said Joanne. 'You're always worrying what things look like. It's what's inside that matters.'

You would say that, I caught myself thinking, and then felt sorry for being such a bitch.

We went through a side door and down a short corridor, then into the room Joanne had mentioned. To be honest, my first thought was: youth club! Same kind of old chairs and tables, all a bit drab, a battered darts board, a pool table. The smell was different, though – stale beer and fag smoke. A bit better than old socks, any rate.

But as we stood there, a door opposite us opened, and everything changed. For the better.

It was Tarik, walking towards us, moving easily, elegant, smiling.

'Joanne! Emma! So glad you could make it.'

We shook hands – he was always formal like that, Tarik, and he led us to a table. 'Sit down,' he said. 'What can I get you?'

Smirnoffs all round. He disappeared out the door, then came back holding a tray with three glasses and a bottle on it.

'This should do us for a start,' he said, very cheerful, pouring the drinks.

We settled back in our seats, and then Tarik said, 'Something to eat? You shouldn't really drink on an empty stomach.'

He was right. That was thoughtful.

'I'll get you some sandwiches,' he said, and went back through the door.

Me and Joanne looked at each other.

'This is a bit of all right,' I said.

'Glad you think so,' she said, smiling. She had a nice smile, Joanne. She didn't show it often enough.

So we drank our drinks, and ate our sandwiches (a bit hard and curling at the edges, but who cares?), while Tarik chatted about his friend's plans for the pub.

'He's got great ideas, Marek has,' he said. 'It's a bit of a dump now, but in six months you won't know it. He'll strip it all out, do it up. He's got an architect to do an extension. Really classy. Good food. Good drink.' Then he smiled directly at us and lifted his glass. 'Good company.'

I'll drink to that.

I was really enjoying myself. Joanne's right, I thought. It doesn't matter what the place is like, it's what's inside. Or, more to the point, who.

A while after we'd eaten, Tarik changed the subject and said to me, 'Emma, fancy a game of pool?'

'Oh,' I said. 'I don't know how to play it.'

'I'll show you,' Tarik said. 'Come on.'

He led me over to one of the pool tables, put a coin in the side of it, and the balls came tumbling out with a lot of noise. He picked up a cue and rubbed a little cube of chalk on one end. Then he showed me how to hold the cue and hit the ball. At one point he was standing right over me, we were both leaning over the table, his hands were moving mine to the right position. I can hardly describe it, but I felt safe. He knew what he was doing, and he was showing me how. He was a good teacher, very patient. I was a bit woozy by now, I must say, and sometimes my eyes were crossing. But he encouraged me all the time. 'Well done, Emma,' he said when a ball actually went into one of the holes, and I felt great.

I had a mad thought – imagine if all the teachers at school were like Tarik! I'd know everything! He was a hero.

Then, just when I'd have been happy to stay in the pub for ever, Tarik looked at his watch (gold, I saw, like Ali's, but much thinner, not so showy), and said, 'Time to go, Emma.'

I was crushed. 'What? Why? I'm having a good time.'

He smiled, still patient. 'Oh, Emma, Emma,' he said. 'You know you have to be home by nine, before your mum and dad come home.' How did he know that? Oh, of course, Joanne must have told him. He's not a mind reader.

He was going on. 'I know nine o'clock is ridiculously early to get home, but if that's what your parents want, that's what you must do.'

'But I haven't finished the game,' I wailed, waving my cue around.

He dodged the cue and took it from me. He put it on the table.

'We'll finish it another day,' he said.

Another day! Oh good, there'll be another day.

He walked me and Joanne to the bus stop, which was really thoughtful, showed he cared about our safety. 'Can't be too careful,' he said. 'You never know who's about.'

No. You never do.

10

Top of My World

'D'you know what, Emma? I know we only met a few weeks ago, but I feel I've known you for years.' Tarik shook his head. 'How about that?' he went on. 'Don't think I've known anyone like you before.' Now he smiled, a big smile. 'Not used to it!' he said, and he raised his glass to me. We were sitting in the back room of the pub. Even this dull, smelly old place brightened up when Tarik was in it.

I smiled back and raised my own glass, though I could've jumped up and down, I was that made up. Only I didn't, of course. I never made it too obvious how struck I was by him. I didn't want him to think I was a silly young girl, all over-excited by glamorous grown-ups, so I acted cool, but friendly at the same time. It must have worked, as he was saying now, 'I tell you, Emma, you might look like a young girl, but you're very mature for your age. There's a lot to you. I feel I can really talk to you.'

Well, I felt ten feet tall. Life doesn't get much better than this, I thought. I'd never met anyone like him, either, I realised that now. At school, I'd hear other girls talking about their so-called boyfriends, boys in our year, and think, What are you like? How can you bother with those boring, spotty little boys? Just giggling, and snogging. I ask you. I'd look at them and I'd feel sorry for them, really. They didn't know what it was like to be friends with a real man of the world, someone who'd done something with his life, who was good-looking, charming, well-off, very sophisticated. Sophisticated – those boys wouldn't know the meaning of the word. Tarik was like James Bond and they were like Bart Simpson. Tarik wasn't my boyfriend, of course, nothing like that, but he was getting more and more special to me.

Not that I talked about him to all and sundry. Not to anyone, really. When I'd first got to know the Asian lads, first at the mall and then in town, I'd chatted about them. They were something new in my life, and not a secret, not something to hide. I even talked about them to Mum and Dad, and they didn't think anything of it. They knew they could rely on me to be sensible, and come home at the right time and all that. In fact, from the way I described Niv and Jay, Mum said, 'They sound like nice lads.

Maybe our Stevie could take a leaf out of their book.'

When the drinking and the dope started, I knew I had to keep a bit of a cover on it, and I talked less and less about my new friends. As far as Mum and Dad were concerned, I was hanging out with my old girl-friends and the lads had just dropped out of sight. So by the time I got to know Tarik, I wasn't in the habit of talking about our times together to anyone outside the group. This meant nearly all the girls at school (I hardly ever spoke to the boys anyway). Just Joanne and Chloe were still in with me, though Chloe wouldn't come out with me if she knew Tarik was going to be on the scene. I couldn't understand this, but knew I just had to accept it if I wanted to go on being friends with her, which I did. My other old friends were going their own way by now too. Claire hadn't joined in for ages, of course, and Sophie wasn't keen now. In fact, she'd said something funny to me just a week before, on the Monday, during break.

'Me and a coupla mates were in mall yesterday,' she said, 'and we saw Joanne.'

'Yeah?' I said. This wasn't news, was it? Joanne liked the mall as much as I did, only I didn't usually go on a Sunday, at least not till after dinner. Mum and Dad had always made sure we ate Sunday dinner together, leaving the shop in Joanie's hands, and now Stevie had left they were still pretty hot on it. I'd been grumbling, but Mum had said, 'Oh, Emma, surely you can manage one meal with us a week?' Afterwards, I'd usually go into town rather than the mall. So I said to Sophie, 'What about it?'

I wasn't being sharp, we were still friendly when we met. I was just puzzled why she was bothering to mention it. And also why she looked so awkward, shifting about on her feet, going red in the face.

'She were with a couple of girls,' Sophie said. 'We were sat on balcony and we saw her walking out with them through main doors.'

'Yeah?' I said again, thinking, Your point is?

Sophie looked me full in the face then, and said, 'Emma, they were young girls, maybe twelve, maybe even younger, first years.'

She still looked at me, as if she was expecting this to mean something. I just thought, Well, why shouldn't she hang out with who she likes? Older, younger...what about it?

When I didn't say anything, must have just looked puzzled, Sophie added, 'I've gotta tell you, Emma. When they went out, they met up with a gang of lads outside doors. We could see them through glass. Asian lads.'

She nodded, as if this should mean something special.

'Well, what about it?' I said. 'She knows a lot of Asian lads – you know she does, you've known some yourself, come to that.'

'Yeah, I know,' she said. 'And it were fun, for a while. But, Emma, think on. Joanne's fourteen, and she looks old for her age. These lads looked older too, not like Niv and Jay. Older than us.'

'So what?' I asked, getting a bit sharp this time. What was she thinking of? 'Come on, Sophie. If you've got owt to say, say it.'

Sophie frowned and said, 'Right. I will. I reckon Joanne is getting young girls to meet those lads. I don't like the look of it.'

'Don't like the look of it? Think there's funny business or what? What's wrong with you, Sophie?' I was getting mardy now. 'She brought us together with a great bunch of lads, didn't she? And you said yourself, it were fun.' And I couldn't resist adding, 'And it still is, for me.' I tried not to look too pleased with myself, showing off.

Sophie just sighed. 'Yeah, I heard you were hanging out with some guy – he nicked Joanne's phone, didn't he?'

'He did not!' I shot back. 'He wouldn't do owt like

that. It were Joanne mucking about, making a scene. You know what she's like.'

'Yeah,' said Sophie again. 'Reckon I do.'

'So is that it?' I demanded. 'Is that what you wanna say?'

Sophie shrugged. 'I thought you wouldn't listen, Emma.'

'Too right I wouldn't,' I said, 'if you're just gonna talk crap.'

'Okay,' she said. 'Well, I tried.' She turned aside to walk off, then stopped and looked me full in the eye. 'Be careful,' she said.

Be careful! I watched her walk off to the canteen and I was gobsmacked. There was a girl who'd known me for years, and she didn't really know me at all. Tarik had only known me for weeks and already he had a better idea of what made me tick. Sophie must be thinking I'm stupid, getting in over my head or something. But I knew what I was doing. I knew Tarik, just like the other guys, wasn't dangerous. They wouldn't try anything on. Well, there was that time Aman tried to take liberties, then Kaz, but they were prats.

What was Sophie suggesting? Tarik wanted to get off with young girls? He was a paedophile? I had a picture in my mind of what a paedo was. We'd all heard about them. A dirty, greasy, middle-aged man, wanting to get his grubby mitts on a little child. Disgusting, sick, no question. Okay, Tarik was in his early twenties, so he might be as much as ten years older than me. But so what? I wasn't a little child, I was a teenager. I'd be fourteen in just a few months. That was the difference, and it was a big difference. If a grown man was hanging out with an eight-year-old, that would be out of order, that would be suspicious. But I was practically grown up, Tarik said so.

I looked over at him now, in the pub, sat easy in his chair. Whatever he did, he made it look easy, effortless.

'Want a game?' he said, nodding over at the pool table.

'Sure,' I said. 'I'm still not much good, though.'

'No matter,' he said. 'You just need practice.'

Like the first time he showed me how to play, he was very patient. Didn't take the mick when I played an awful shot, not even if the ball bounced right off the table and rolled along the floor. That made his mates laugh and groan at the same time.

'Don't listen to them,' Tarik said. 'They're idiots.'

They didn't take offence, as far as I could tell. It was like banter. I'd met them some time before, Jakko and Zane. Jakko specially was always around, as he drove Tarik where he wanted to go. I'd been surprised when I found out Tarik didn't drive his car himself. Was Jakko a kind of chauffeur, then? I wondered. That's posh! But Tarik told me, 'A small disagreement with the law.' That was probably drink-driving, then. Bad luck.

Tarik's car was one of those big fancy ones where you can hardly hear the engine. A BMW like Ali's, I think. Jakko was a nice enough guy, if a bit slow on the uptake sometimes. The thing you noticed most about him was how tall he was, at least a head taller than Tarik. The other mate, Zane, was quiet, with a soft voice, didn't have much to say for himself. I think he looked up to Tarik – like Jakko, he was all ready to jump if Tarik said jump. Not that he often did that, he was too well mannered to order people about.

Now Tarik was saying, 'Well done! Good shot,' as one of the balls I'd hit actually went down a hole. I was very aware of him close by me. He didn't get too close, kept some distance, but it was like the air between us was sparking, tingling. He always wore the same scent, quite a heavy sort of cologne, I suppose. It couldn't be aftershave, as he had a beard. On the other hand, it was one of those very fine beards, thin strips, so maybe he shaved the bits in between and put aftershave there. I don't know. I did ask him once what the scent was.

He said a word that didn't mean anything to me, and added, 'It's a special blend, heavy on the musk. D'you like it?'

'Um…' I said. To be honest, it practically made my eyes water, but somehow it suited him, strong and a bit unsettling. I came to associate it with him. In fact, I was once in the mall, browsing round Superdrug, when I caught a whiff of the scent and immediately thought, 'Tarik!' I turned round with a smile on my face, only to find an old fat man, dressed in that traditional costume Muslims wear, long white jacket and baggy white trousers. I think he was surprised by this strange girl grinning away at him.

I wondered why Tarik and his mates never wore this traditional costume. It didn't look much good on this man in the shop, but I'd seen other men wearing it and they really stood out, sort of exotic and dignified at the same time.

'Oh, I wouldn't be seen dead in it,' said Tarik. 'That's for old men. Old life, old ways. If I went around wearing it I'd never be taken seriously in business. People would think I was straight off the boat.'

I guessed he meant arriving as an immigrant, and

it wasn't a good image. From little things he said, I gathered he'd been born here in England, and looked down on people who'd just arrived, especially if they stuck to their old ways, how they dressed, how they spoke.

'What sort of business?' I asked, straight out. I must say I'd been curious what Tarik did for a living. Like Ali, he was obviously doing well, and I felt I knew him well enough to ask.

Tarik looked at me with one eyebrow raised, which he often did.

'D'you really want to know?' he asked. 'It's really boring. I do it and I do it well, but even I find it boring.'

'What?' I asked.

'It's import-export,' he said. 'People make stuff, people buy stuff, and I'm the man in the middle.'

'What sort of stuff?'

He waved a hand. 'Oh, you name it,' he said. 'You know that big shop in town, next to the butcher's, where they sell everything?'

I knew the one he meant – I'd gone round it quite a few times, boggled at how much was stacked on the shelves. If I'd thought my mum and dad's shop was stuffed full – well! Here there was everything from cups and saucers to screwdrivers and toilet sets, toys and envelopes and brightly coloured china ornaments that I thought were hideous. So much stuff!

'That's what you deal in?' I asked.

'Yeah. Told you – boring.' Then he smiled. 'But profitable.'

I was impressed. 'Dunno how you keep track of everything,' I said.

'With difficulty,' he said. Then, 'That's enough talk about business. I like to get away from it. Fancy a drink?'

Maybe it was because I showed an interest in his work that Tarik asked me to help him. That, plus the fact he knew he could trust me to be sensible.

It was a couple of days after we'd been in the pub and played pool. We'd met up at the war memorial in the evening, and he asked me to walk with him to his car. It was parked a way up the street, and Jakko was sitting in the driver's seat. We got in the back, and Tarik reached into his inside jacket pocket. He got out an envelope, about the size of a birthday card, only thicker.

'Emma,' he said, 'can I ask you to do me a favour?'

A favour? Like a shot, so I said, "Course you can. What is it?'

He didn't say anything for a moment, just tapped the envelope he was holding. Then he said, 'I need to get this to someone tonight. It's a contract on some stuff I've ordered. The thing is, it's a bit tricky.'

I was all ears. 'What's the problem?'

'To be honest, I don't want anybody else to know about it. If I'm seen with this guy, certain people will put two and two together and the deal's off. I could ask Jakko here to take it, or Zane, but everybody knows they're in with me. I don't want to raise any suspicions. See what I mean?'

I could see, straight away. 'Well, they won't know me, will they?'

'Exactly,' said Tarik, with one of his big smiles. 'Sorry about the cloak and dagger business – but that's what it is. Business. Cut-throat competition, you know. I want this deal tied up tonight, and eyes are everywhere.'

I was pleased as anything. I felt a glow that he could trust me with something so important. I knew he was right about business being tough. 'Sharks out there,' I'd heard my dad say. 'Gobble you up as soon as look at you.' I knew how hard he and Mum had to work to make a success of the shop with everyone wanting to cut down their profit margins.

'Where do I take it?' I asked.

'I'll show you,' he said. Then, 'Okay, Jakko.'

The car moved away and we went through a few streets till we got near to a patch of waste ground.

'See that red car over there?' asked Tarik.

He was nodding at a car parked all by itself, up the road. It was another of those big cars, but in the dim light I couldn't tell what colour it was.

'Yeah.'

'Just tap on the driver's window, and when he opens it, pass this through.' He gave me the envelope.

'Do I say owt?'

'No, no need. He'll know who it's from.'

'Right then.' I started getting out and for a moment Tarik pressed my hand.

'Thanks, Emma, you're a star.'

I practically floated down the street to the car, and tapped on the window. It opened straight away, and the driver put out his hand. I couldn't see much of the rest of him, he was all muffled up, except I could tell he was black. He didn't say a word, just flashed me a grin that showed a gold tooth, took the envelope and rolled the window up.

As I walked back to Tarik's car, I thought, This is like a film. I'm a spy delivering secret plans. How cool is that? Even if the plans were more like an order for toilet seats, for all I knew.

Back in the car, Tarik was all smiles and thanks. 'You've saved my life,' he said.

And right off I thought to myself, I'd do anything for you.

11

Friends and Enemies

'I can't,' I said. 'I'm going out.'

Mum and Dad both stopped stuffing their faces with eggs and bacon and stared at me.

'What d'you mean?' asked Mum. 'You always work in shop on Fridays.'

'Well, I don't now,' I said. 'I've had enough of that poxy shop.'

'What?' Bits of food burst out of Dad's mouth. 'That poxy shop, as you call it, keeps food on the table and clothes on your back, our Emma, and don't you forget it.'

Same old story, I thought. Heard it all before.

Mum went on in a quieter voice. 'Where did this come from, Emma? You've not said owt about not wanting to work in shop. What's got into you?'

'Nothing,' I said, sharp. 'I'm just sick and tired of going there every week. I've got better things to do, me.'

'Better things? What better things?' said Dad. He was really annoyed, I could tell. His face always went red. 'Going out with your precious mates, I suppose.'

'Well, yeah, as it happens,' I shot back. And that was true. Me and Joanne were going to meet Tarik and his mates in the pub, and have a proper meal out.

When Tarik suggested it the other day, I'd told him about working in the shop.

'Yes,' he said, 'I do remember you mentioned it. But surely they don't expect you to work every Friday, if you want to go out somewhere?'

I hadn't really thought about it. 'Um, yeah, I think they do.'

'What?' he said, looking right surprised. 'Every Friday? At the end of a week at school? Well, it's your business, I suppose, but that doesn't seem very fair to me.'

Now I came to think of it, it didn't sound fair to me either.

'Do they pay you?' Tarik went on.

'Yeah, a tenner.'

His eyebrows rose further up. 'A tenner? Is that all? For three hours, you say?'

I didn't mention the bit about popping upstairs to see Nan in time for *Emmerdale* and the rest. I liked it that Tarik was obviously feeling concerned on my account.

He was shaking his head. 'Well, I call that cheap. I know they're your mum and dad, Emma, and you're still at school, but I call it taking a liberty. And a Friday too – that's just the evening everyone wants off at the end of the week. Well, I mean, you can stay out late as you don't have to get up in the morning, do you?'

That was true, so I nodded.

'I know there's Saturday night,' Tarik said, 'but even then you have to be back by nine, don't you?'

'Yeah,' I said. 'Mum and Dad like me to be home when they get back from work.'

Tarik shook his head again. 'What are they like?' he said. 'Treating you like a kid – you have to leave just when things are warming up, don't you?'

That was true too. I always had to keep an eye on the time, and I'd often had to drag myself away just when folk were getting mellow, there was a good vibe going. Joanne had had a go at me a couple of times recently.

'Come on, Emma, just stay another half-hour.'

'I can't.'

'Why not?'

'You know why not. I gotta be back. Mum and Dad'll go spare.'

She made her 'Doh' noise. 'Oh, Mum and Dad, we

can't have them going spare, can we? Well, if you're late, what can they do?'

That made me think.

'I dunno,' I said. 'Maybe they'd ground me. Stop my pocket money.'

'That's so unfair,' Joanne said. 'You're entitled to enjoy yourself.'

I thought so too. I wished my parents were more like hers – they wouldn't care if Joanne got in at midnight, she'd told me so.

Now Tarik was saying, 'I thought it would be nice to take you and Joanne out for a meal on Friday. Jakko could drive us somewhere nice. Why don't you tell your mum and dad you've got plans?'

So there I was at breakfast Friday morning, facing Mum and Dad and telling them no way was I working at the shop that evening.

For a minute nobody said anything. Then Dad put his knife and fork down and looked straight at me.

'It's not like we're asking much of you, Emma,' he said. 'It doesn't hurt you to help out just one evening a week. Me and your mum—'

'Work seven days a week,' I snapped. 'Yeah, yeah, don't I know it.'

Mum looked shocked. She put her knife and fork down too.

'Emma, what's got into you? You mustn't speak to us like that.'

'Why not?'

'Cos we're your parents,' Dad put in, a big frown on his face. 'You owe us some respect.'

'And you owe me respect!' I burst out. 'Treating me like a kid and telling me I have to be back just when everyone else starts enjoying themselves. People laugh at me cos of you!'

Now they were both staring at me as if they'd never seen me before. Well, I thought, maybe they haven't. All they've seen is a little kid who has to be looked after, they haven't noticed I'm growing up.

That's another thing Tarik said to me. He's a very observant person, I always thought. He sees things other folk don't.

'People have mindsets,' he told me. 'They make their minds up about something and stick to it. Nothing makes them change. I reckon that's what's happened with your mum and dad. They've got so used to you being their sweet little girl that they don't realise you're growing up, you're capable of thinking for yourself. You've got your head screwed on, all right. You don't need them fussing and flapping as if you're still ten years old.'

Well, he was spot on there.

'There's another thing,' he said, 'and I hope you don't mind me mentioning it, Emma. I only say it because I care about you—' Straight off it flashed through my mind. He cares about me! He's said it! Then he was going on. 'Maybe your parents haven't noticed you've changed because they just don't see much of you, do they? There's no one at home when you get back, and it's you waiting for them to come home. Do they really have to work all those hours?'

I must have looked surprised, as he added, 'Oh, don't get me wrong. I'm all for working long hours. Every Indian and Pakistani shopkeeper does that. But do you think they just might be working in the shop so much because they like it that way? Not having to be with you?'

Now that did shock me. I'd never thought of it like that.

'I'm sure they didn't start doing it on purpose,' he said. 'But they got in the way of it, and never wanted to change, to spend more time at home with you. I wonder why not?' He smiled straight at me. 'Who wouldn't want to spend time with you?'

That made me laugh. If it was anybody else, I'd have said he was flirting, but him and me didn't do that. I was realising more and more that we had a special kind of bond that was streets away from ordinary boyfriend and girlfriend stuff. I guess I was building him up as my hero, simple as that.

But who could blame me, when he cared about me, took such an interest. I always wondered if it was the way Muslims were brought up, to be very polite and not talk about themselves. The ones I knew always asked you about yourself, encouraged you to talk about your life, even ordinary everyday stuff. About school, about your family, what they did, where they went. It was putting other people first, which, come to think of it, Mum and Dad were always going on about. Well, they should approve, then.

It was because Tarik was so kind to me that I was very happy to do something for him in return, running errands in town. 'You're my personal delivery service,' he said to me, and that made me proud. After that first delivery a couple of weeks back, he'd asked me several times to take an envelope, or a small package, to some guy or other in town. Sometimes he was in a shop, sometimes in a car again. I wasn't to make a song and dance about it – you never knew who might be watching. I thought how hard business must be for him, when he had to watch his back all the time. Good job he had people he could trust, like me. I enjoyed being useful to him – it beat working in the shop! Not that I thought of it as work, it was just doing a favour for a friend. And there wasn't any payment. As it was, Tarik was generous, buying me fags and vodka, and spliffs now and then. But I didn't want to take advantage of his good nature.

And now I was seeing my mum and dad at the breakfast table through Tarik's eyes. Because of him, I could see them clearly. They were so selfish, putting themselves first, not paying any attention to what I wanted. All that talk about working so hard for all the family, so we had nice things – that was crap. Why hadn't I seen it before? They were suiting themselves, that's all. And another thing – they didn't trust me, did they? How could they, when they wouldn't let me stay out later than nine o'clock, for God's sake? What did they think I was going to do? Run off with a guy? Get myself in trouble? Is that what they thought of me? I felt really angry with them, and angry at myself too for being so blind and stupid. They'd pulled the wool over my eyes all right. Maybe Stevie had seen through them, that's why he wanted to leave home. He wouldn't stay where he wasn't wanted. Now I knew I wasn't wanted either.

'You can stuff your bloody shop!'

Dad stood up so fast his chair fell over backwards. I'd never seen him look so angry.

'Just you listen to me, young lady! he yelled.

That's rich, I thought. Young lady. He doesn't think I'm a young lady, he thinks I'm a young girl.

Mum was on her feet too, putting a hand on Dad's arm.

'Calm down, Jason,' she said. 'I'll handle this.'

Then she looked at me and said, 'Emma, I want a word with you. Come into front room.'

'I'll be late for school,' I said, just wanting to spoil whatever she had in mind.

'No you won't,' Mum said. 'You've plenty of time, and this won't wait.'

I dragged my feet into the front room, and flung myself down on one of the armchairs. 'What?' I practically spat it out.

Mum sat down opposite, and looked straight at me.

'Now, Emma,' she said. 'I can see you're upset, and I don't know why—'

'You don't know owt!' I burst out, and scrunched down with my arms folded. It was like I wanted a barrier between us.

Mum was still sat there calm. 'That's as maybe,' she said. 'I've never pretended to be mastermind. But I do know there's summat up, and I want to help you.'

Help me! As if.

She was going on. 'I know you're at a difficult age,

love. You feel all mixed up, and angry. Believe it or not, I can remember being a teenager meself. But there's ways through it, Emma, and taking on at your mum and dad in't one of them. We've always talked, haven't we? So what's to stop us talking now?'

Oh God, I wasn't going to fall for this soft soap. I scrambled up off the chair and said, 'I'm not listening to this. I'm off.'

I stomped off and turned round at the door.

'And if you think I'll be seen dead in that shop you've got another think coming. I'm going out tonight and that's that!'

As I went into the hall, I could hear Mum following me, calling out. 'Emma. Take care. Please be back by nine o'clock.'

I slammed the front door, which made me feel very satisfied.

'You told them, then. Told them pretty good.' Tarik was smiling. Maybe that was pride in his face, I thought. I felt pretty good myself, smoking a fag, sipping my drink.

'Yeah, about time too,' said Joanne.

'Oh, don't blame Emma,' said Tarik. 'I know her. It's not in her nature to put herself forward.' Then he looked at me. 'There just comes a time when you have to stand up for yourself. Know yourself, and know who your friends are.'

I know my friends all right, I thought. Looking round that back room in the pub, I didn't see the old furniture, none of it matching, or the mouldy old dartboard, or the torn covering of the pool table. I saw friends. This is where I belonged. Wherever they were, that's where I belonged. I felt as if I was glowing, and I was getting choked, my throat closing up.

Maybe something showed in my face, as Tarik leaned forward and touched my arm.

'It can be upsetting, I know,' he said, 'when you have to take on your parents. But don't forget, Emma, they're the grown-ups, aren't they? They should be the ones knowing what's what. They should be looking out for you, but I reckon they've been taking you for granted. It's not my idea of love.' And he sat back.

Love. That was the first time I'd ever heard him say that word. Did he feel love for me? Not like a dad for a daughter, that would be mad. More like an uncle and niece, maybe. Or an older cousin for a younger cousin. That was more like it. Friendship, but with something extra in it, a tie that bound us.

I realised that he thought I was welling up because I'd had a go at my parents. Though he usually knew the truth of things, this one time he was wrong, but only because he didn't like to see me upset, he was trying to comfort me. I wondered what he'd think if I just came out with what was in my head.

'I love you and I love all my friends and I don't give a damn for my bloody mum and dad.'

I was all for staying out till all hours – 'That'll show 'em,' I said. But Tarik knew better than that.

'Think of it long term, Emma. It's what we do in business. We call it strategy. You don't act on impulse, just cos you feel like it. It'll screw things up in the long run. If you get back late tonight, your mum and dad'll be on your mobile before you know what's happening.'

'I'll turn it off,' I said, straight out.

Tarik smiled. 'Well, they'd still be waiting for you when you got in, wouldn't they? And you have to go home some time.'

That was true, I supposed.

He was going on. 'Believe me, it's best for you to do what they say. For now, anyway. It wouldn't hurt you to say sorry, either, for carrying on.'

'Sorry!' I said. 'I'm not sorry.'

'I know you're not,' said Tarik. 'But act like you are, and they won't know, will they? While you're under their roof, you have to play ball. Remember, it's strategy.'

Strategy. Sounded impressive. And I could see the sense in it.

'Maybe,' I said. I was seeing pictures in my head, real and colourful. Must be the weed. I saw myself being nice, and Mum and Dad being taken in, when all the time I'd be doing what I wanted... This made me laugh out loud.

Tarik cocked an eyebrow. 'Well, I'm glad you've cheered up, Emma. Tell you what, Jakko'll run you back, okay? That'll save you hanging around for a bus. You'll have time for another drink.'

Sounded good to me. I wondered where the proper meal had got to, that Tarik had mentioned. We'd just been eating crisps. But it didn't matter. Company was more important than food, and now I had a ride home. Good. I could play this game.

Until it stopped being a game.

12

True Colours

That day started just like any other. I can't pretend I had a funny feeling, a sense that something was going to happen to me. Life was just ordinary. In the weeks leading up to it, I'd been trying to stick to what Tarik said, about behaving myself at home. But it wasn't easy. I made sure I was always back when Mum and Dad said, and did my bit in the shop on Fridays – and it was dead busy before Christmas. Still bored me stiff, though. I found myself snapping at everyone. I was even sharp with my nan, who I'd always got on with so well. But it was like folk were forever rubbing me up the wrong way. Everything they said was getting at me. In the end I avoided everybody as much as I could.

This was tricky at Christmas, what with people coming round. At least Stevie was back home on holiday – 'You get great holidays on oil rig,' he'd told us. 'Weeks on, weeks off.' Which cheered Mum up. I thought maybe I could talk to him, let off some steam about Mum and Dad and everything that was shit and unfair in my life. But no chance. I hardly saw him – he was off with his mates every minute he could, having a high old time. We had Nan and Auntie Sue over for Christmas Day dinner, and I can't say I was the life and soul.

'Summat up, pet?' asked my nan in the afternoon as I slumped in front of the telly with the rest of them.

'No, I'm all right,' I said. And nobody asked me again.

I did hear Stevie, though, when I was on the landing and he was going into the kitchen.

'What's up with our Emma?' he was asking Mum and Dad. 'Got a proper face on her.'

'Oh, leave it, lad,' said Mum. 'She's having a hard time.'

Stevie made a rude noise. 'Hard? She should try oil rig!'

Yeah, I thought. And you should try my life.

Then Christmas was over, thank God, and I hoped things would get back to normal. I'd told Tarik that I had to stay round home over Christmas, and he understood, as he always did.

'We're the same about Eid,' he said. 'It's a special time for us.'

Before the school holidays were up, me and Chloe managed another Saturday in the mall. Joanne was off somewhere, so it was just us. The mall was still busy, as the sales were on, and we grabbed a few bargains. We wandered about as usual, and made our way to the amusement arcade. It was packed too, with a lot of Asian lads in there. All the time folk were saying, 'Hi, Emma, hi, Chloe,' and we were smiling back, with 'Happy New Year' and all that.

It was only when we were outside, heading for McDonald's, when a thought suddenly hit me.

'D'you know, Chloe,' I said, 'we must have known every single Asian lad in arcade. I don't think there was one what didn't say hello.'

Chloe raised her eyebrows. 'Reckon you're right. Just shows what good taste they've got.'

I don't know why I had that thought just then. I knew that they all knew each other, what with so many of them being related. I suppose I just hadn't realised how many we'd got to know – or at least to say hello to. I liked it. It made me feel connected to a sort of big web of people. It was something I'd never felt about kids at school or our neighbours in the village. It was how you should feel about your family, I thought.

Anyway, me and Chloe enjoyed ourselves, and I

thought again how easy she was to get along with, not like Joanne. After the shops shut we made our way to the side of the building, to the delivery yard. Lorries were in and out all day, but everything was quiet after closing time. It was only when we started staying out later that we found out about this place – it was a nice quiet spot to have a couple of joints, round a corner and well out the way.

Chloe passed a spliff to me, and I gave her some money. That was another reason to behave myself, of course – keep getting my pocket money. I didn't want to ponce off Chloe and Joanne all the time. We sat down on a couple of old boxes and blew smoke into the evening air. Perfect peace. Then Chloe got the giggles and I knew it was time to go. I thought a lot of Chloe, but I didn't want to have to practically drag her to the bus stop when she was out of it. I knew we shouldn't attract attention – you never knew who might be looking. Someone might recognise me, and word would get back to Mum and Dad. That didn't bear thinking about.

We were going to Chloe's for our tea, and when we got in she was laughing that loud I was having to shush her up. 'Your mum'll hear you,' I whispered.

'Oh, she won't notice,' said Chloe, wobbling about. 'She never does. Just spends her time with her head in pots.' This set her off again, and I wasn't surprised to hear her mum call from the kitchen, where she seemed to spend most of her time.

'You girls all right?'

'Yeah, yeah,' I called. 'Just having a laugh.' That was true.

I don't know how I got Chloe upstairs so she could crash out and recover. She kept waving a finger and saying, 'Don't let her see your eyes, don't let her see your eyes. Keep your head down...' She had a thing about the pupils of your eyes getting bigger when you were smoking dope. 'Dead giveaway,' she said.

I look back on that evening now, and it's a lovely memory. The laughs, the mucking about, the warmth, the tasty food Chloe's mum cooked.

It was four days before everything changed.

We'd arranged to meet the Wednesday after we went back to school. Or to put it another way, Joanne had told me Tarik would like us to meet up, in town.

'He'll meet us off bus,' she said.

This was great, another sign that Tarik was looking out for us. I saw him the minute the bus swung into the station. It stopped in C block, which was a way from the other parking places, and I recognised Tarik leaning against one of the shelters, smoking a fag. There were two other men with him, who I didn't recognise.

He greeted me and Joanne with a smile, and introduced his friends.

'This is Azad and this is Imran,' he said. The men grinned back at us, and I must say I didn't think that much of them. They were older, for a start, quite a bit older, well into their thirties as far as I could tell. They were bigger than Tarik, taller and wider. They weren't badly dressed or dirty or anything ugly like that. They just didn't have Tarik's style. I wondered how he knew them, then reminded myself he seemed to know everyone. And the men kept grinning, which was a bit off-putting. At least they seemed pleased to see us.

'Well, ladies,' Tarik was saying. 'Where shall we go this evening?' Then he answered his own question. 'What about the war memorial – or the club, as they call it. That's more like it. Haven't been there for a while.'

I'd been hoping he'd say the Red Lion, or maybe a ride in a car. It was really chilly now, nearly the middle of January, and I was wishing I'd put on a thick coat instead of my white plastic one. Still, we'd be out of the wind, and it was very private there.

So me and Joanne nodded, and off we strolled, Tarik between me and Joanne, the two other men behind. We didn't talk much. By the time we reached the market and went round the side, I wanted the toilet. 'Won't be a minute,' I said, and headed towards one we often used, a disabled toilet with a broken lock. Joanne came along with me to stand outside and keep folk out.

Just as I opened the door and put the light on, I felt a sudden push in the middle of my back and I stumbled into the little room. Out of nowhere, Tarik was beside me, pushing me up against the wall. His friend Azad was beside him, still grinning.

'What're you doing?' I burst out, more surprised than anything. This wasn't like Tarik, who was usually so polite and kept his distance. 'Leave off!'

Tarik just laughed, and pressed me against the wall with his whole body. He must be drunk, or drugged, I thought, but I'm not standing for this.

'Joanne!' I shouted.

'Why?' Tarik said. 'What d'you think she'll do?'

'Join in,' said Azad, and they both laughed.

Now I was getting scared, trying to push Tarik off. In a moment he'd stepped back, saying, 'Emma, Emma, don't take on. I were only having a laugh. Can't you take a joke?'

Well, that was not my idea of a joke. I was a bit shaken, and still had to go to the toilet.

'You get out of here,' I said, and called out to Joanne to stand outside.

'Don't worry, don't worry,' Tarik said. 'It's all yours.'

By the time I got out, they were all lounging about, smoking.

'At last,' said Tarik. 'Emma, there's something I want to show you.'

One of his friends made a funny noise, like a snort. Tarik went on. 'Have you been through that big gate in the yard? It leads up to a walkway – you get a good view.'

I hadn't been there, and wondered what we could see in this light. There were just a few streetlamps around, so I could make out his face, as good-humoured as ever. He seemed back to his charming self. I felt a bit silly for making a fuss, and said, 'Sure, whatever.'

The gate in the yard wasn't locked, it turned out. I'd always noticed the thick chain through it, but when I looked closely, I realised there was no padlock on it.

'Up we go,' said Tarik. 'Ladies first.'

The gate opened with a screeching noise and we saw a set of concrete steps ahead of us. Me and Joanne climbed up, then we were out on a walkway. I hadn't noticed this from the ground. I'd always thought there were solid brick walls around, but this was sort of set into one wall. Not much view, I must say. As far as I could see in the light, it was just a bit of a wasteland, a few burnt-out cars, lots of weeds and rubbish.

'Keep going,' said Tarik. 'Follow it round.'

So we walked round – and came to a dead end. It was like a small room, with a door set into one wall, with metal railings over it. There was litter blowing about on the ground, and a smell of something I couldn't place, but it wasn't nice. And definitely not worth looking at. I suddenly shivered, and Tarik was right next to me.

'Something wrong?' he asked.

'I'm right cold,' I said, pushing my hands deep into my pockets.

'Here,' he said, 'let me warm you up.'

'No, I'm all right,' I said, but he put his arms around me and held me close. I could smell his musky scent, very strong, and feel his breath on my hair. My mind was a whirl. I didn't know what to think. Was he just being kind, or was he trying it on? I couldn't believe he was trying it on – he just wasn't interested in me that way.

I soon knew different.

Before I knew what was happening, he grabbed my shoulders and pushed me down on to the ground. Then he was on me.

When I think about that time, and it's burned in my mind, it's like seeing it in slow motion, in a film. That's me, lying on the dirty ground with a man on top of me. I look very small, lying there, very pale in the dim light. Another man is holding my wrists, pulling my arms out behind me. He's holding my wrists in one hand, undoing his trousers with the other. He's getting out his privates, and pushing them close to my face. I'm twisting my head, wild to get away, panic filling my mind. The man on top of me is unzipping my coat, and grabbing the top of my jeans, just pulling the seams apart so they split. Then he's dragging them down, along with my knickers. He's laughing at my socks, my new candy-striped ankle socks, and pulling them off too. Now I've got nothing on my bottom half. I'm trying to kick, to knee him, but there's his whole weight on me. He's pushing up my jersey and shirt, pushing up my bra so I'm all exposed. There's a rushing noise in my head, my heart is beating so hard, and there's another noise, a screaming. That's me. Then the man on top of me is pushing my legs apart, he's forcing himself into me.

The pain is so bad, it's torture, a tearing pain that burns and burns. My screaming gets very high. I jerk my head about to get away from that other man. I won't let him get in my mouth. And I see another thing. Flashes of light, popping on and off. Then what's that face? It's Joanne, but not like I've seen her before. She's being held by a man, her arms behind her back. Another man has his hands on her face, and he's…he's holding her eyes open, with his thumbs and fingers. I can see the white of her eyes, and her eyes are huge. All the time men are laughing, laughing. 'Go on, Tarik! Get in there!' they're saying, and laughing more than ever. More flashes of light. And more pain. Just as he's tearing me up inside, his hands are clawing at my back, my bum, my legs, the inside of my thighs. He's using his nails, his beautiful manicured nails, to scratch me like a cat. I can feel blood all over me, warm and slippery, he's wiping it over my body, my clothes.

My whole world is exploding into pain, more pain, and shock and terror.

That's what it's like to be raped.

And it wasn't the worst that could happen.

13

The End of My World

'You'll be all right, Emma, you'll be all right.'

That was Joanne's voice. It cut through the noise in my head. It must be her hand on my shoulder.

I was crouching on the ground, curled up, my arms wrapped over my head. As soon as Tarik had finished what he was doing and got off me, I'd whipped up my knickers and jeans, and pulled my top clothes down, to cover myself up. It was the only thing I was thinking of, to cover myself. That done, I was frozen, couldn't move. My heart was hammering, and I could hardly breathe. The shock was flooding over me and through me.

'Come on, Emma.' Joanne's voice again. 'You'll catch your death. You gotta move.'

She was pulling my coat round me, then putting my trainers on my feet, tying the laces. 'I put your socks in your bag,' she said. 'They're too fiddly to get on.'

Socks? I remember the word echoing in my head.

Socks? Oh yeah, Tarik pulled them off. He was laughing. 'Little socks for little girls,' he'd said.

Now Joanne was helping me to my feet. But as I tried to stand, I doubled up. I was clutching my stomach as if I was afraid my insides would fall out. The smell of Tarik's scent was in my nose, and I wanted to be sick, but nothing would come up. I was burning all over, and inside too. I'm trying to remember what I thought then, but it's like a blur, all confusion.

Then a thought hit me. 'I need a fag,' I said. That's it, that'll calm my nerves.

Joanne got one straight off, and lit it for me, and put it in my mouth. I dragged on it and the smoke flowed through me. That's when I started to shake, I couldn't help myself. And that's when I started crying. I hadn't cried till now, but now I started, I couldn't stop. I guess I was getting hysterical.

Joanne put an arm round me and hugged me. 'You'll be all right,' she said again. 'Come on, let's get you to toilet and clean you up.'

Clean. That word got through. I must get clean. I felt as if I was dripping with Tarik's stuff. I felt as if I had slime all over me.

With Joanne's help I hobbled along the walkway and down the steps. Then I stopped dead. Why hadn't I thought this before?

'Where is he?' I whispered.

'Don't worry,' said Joanne. 'He's gone off with his mates.'

Right. I'd be safe then.

We reached the toilet, and Joanne put on the light. I staggered over to the basin and looked in the mirror. The face staring back at me was small and white, very white. Joanne was pulling off yards of toilet paper from the roll and bunching it up, then wetting it with soap and water.

'Stand still, Emma,' she said. 'I'll try and get this off your coat.'

Then I noticed just how much blood there was on the white coat, all smeared over. My blood. Joanne opened the coat and my other clothes were a mess too. Where had all that blood come from?

Then I remembered. Tarik had scratched me with his nails, driven them into my skin. Then there was the rough ground I was lying on, what he'd pushed me into. Concrete, bits of grit, rubbing on my bare skin, making it bleed. And he'd wiped the blood over me. There was the other blood too, of course, from inside me. I could feel it trickling down between my legs. I'd heard that virgins bleed when they first have sex, something inside them breaks. That must be it, then.

'That's best I can do,' Joanne was saying, zipping my coat back up.

I looked down at my coat. She'd done a good job. The red was now a pale smudgy pink, it hardly showed. We couldn't do anything about my other clothes, though. That'd have to wait till I got home.

Home. I had to get home.

Joanne held my arm as we left the toilet. She was carrying my bag as well as her own. I managed to walk for a bit, but as the cold night air hit me I felt I was back in that place, and I started to choke. Tarik had been so heavy, I thought he'd crush my chest, push all the air out of my body. My legs went and I fell on the ground, the tears streaming down my face again.

Joanne was beside herself.

'Emma, Emma, we gotta crack on,' she said, shaking my arm. She was that agitated. I just felt so tired that I could've passed out on the concrete, but she pulled me up. Got a tissue out of her pocket and wiped my eyes.

'You don't want folks seeing you crying,' she said. 'They'll know summat's up, and they'll ask questions. You don't want that.'

I tried to breathe steady, and after a while the tears stopped.

'That's better,' said Joanne, and took my arm again.

'Can I have a fag?' I asked.

''Course.' And she lit another one for me, and one for herself. I forced my legs to move and we walked up towards the main road. Just as we turned the corner, I took one look ahead and froze. There was a group of men standing about, leaning against a wall. It was Tarik and his mates.

'Oh no,' I heard myself saying, and my throat closed up.

'Keep going,' Joanne hissed in my ear. 'They can't do nowt in street. There's folks about. Just keep going.'

She held my arm tighter and practically pushed me along. Don't look at them, I told myself. Look straight ahead.

We were just level with them when Tarik stepped forward.

'Emma,' he said, in that voice I'd thought was strong and smooth. Now it was like a knife twisting in my heart. 'Emma. How nice to see you again.'

There were laughs from the other men. Take no notice, I told myself.

He came nearer, and stood right in front of us, so we had to stop.

He was looking me up and down.

'I see you're smoking,' he said. He had a big smile on his face. 'You know what they say, don't you?'

I wasn't going to rise to it. I kept my eyes fixed away from him. He went on. 'They say that when you have a cigarette after sex it means you didn't enjoy it. Did you know that, Emma?'

I still said nothing. He put his face close to mine, and I had to look at him then, but I didn't look at his eyes. I kept my face set.

'Didn't you enjoy it, Emma?' he said, one eyebrow raised. 'I'm sorry if you didn't. Me, I enjoyed it.'

More laughs from his mates.

'And when I see you again, we'll take up where we left off, shall we?'

He stepped back, and joined in the laughter. Joanne pushed me forward, said, 'Come on, we got a bus to catch.'

As we moved off, I could hear Tarik's voice behind us.

'You take care of her, Joanne. You take good care.'

Joanne didn't say anything back, just marched on to the bus station. When we got off the bus, she walked me up to my house.

'You all right?' she said.

I didn't know what to say, just shrugged.

'Look, Emma,' she said, 'I know that were horrible,

but it's over. Don't say owt about it, it'll go away. You'll be all right. See you tomorrow, okay?'

She squeezed my arm, and turned round to go back down the road.

I dragged my feet up the path and opened the door. That's when I heard Mum and Dad's voices. Panic! They're back early. The one night they get back early, and I'm like this.

So when they called to me, I lied about going to the youth club, and how I needed a bath after getting all sweaty. Mum and Dad probably thought I'd been playing table tennis. If there was a moment when I might have burst out about what had happened, it passed, and I made my way upstairs. I knew what I had to do now. Hide everything.

After taking my dirty, bloody clothes off, and packing them carefully away in my wardrobe, I got to the bathroom at last. I locked the door, put the plug in the bath and turned on the taps. Water came gushing out, and steam rose from the stream of hot water. I poured in a good dollop of my favourite bath essence, jasmine, and breathed in the sweet smell. I breathed it in hard. I wanted rid of that other smell, that stink, that scent Tarik used.

Lying in the hot scented water, I tried to relax, to stop my arms and legs twitching about. I breathed deeply, in and out, and some of the tension began to leave me. But at the same time, the pain was coming back. Every bruise was hurting, every scratch, and there was a burning, burning pain deep inside me. I was crying again now, not making much noise, but I could feel the tears spreading over my face, getting lost in the bath water.

Never mind the pain, though – I had to get clean. I scrubbed every inch of me, again and again. I gritted my teeth as I wiped out all the dirt, all the blood. At last my skin, and my hair, was clean as clean, but still that smell hung about. It's in your mind, I told myself. No way could any smell still be hanging about. I had to hold myself together, had to cope.

I remembered to tidy up the bathroom as usual, wiping the bath, spreading out the damp towels over the heated rail, mopping up some spilled water. I knew everything had to look the same. I had to do what I always did. I still looked the same, at least while I was wearing my pyjamas and dressing gown, covered up, no bruises or scratches showing. In the mirror my face might be a bit paler than usual, but it was still the same old Emma. Nobody would know from looking at me that I was different.

And I was different, inside my head and my heart, where it didn't show. I didn't know straight away. It kind of grew on me. Nothing was going to be the same again.

The bruises faded, the scratches healed up – I've always been a quick healer, on account of being healthy, Mum always said. And as the bruises faded and the scratches healed, the pain in my body went away too. Once upon a time, I would've thought, Right, that's it. You get hurt, you get better. That's how it works. But this time, this new time, there was a different sort of pain, that didn't go away. I felt it in my stomach, sure, like it was scrunching up, but I think that's because it was my nerves acting up. I knew in my mind and in my heart what this new pain was, where it came from. I couldn't have put a name to it then, but later I could.

Betrayal.

I would never have guessed that when your world's tumbling down, you could carry on as usual. But it wasn't like I had a big sign on my back saying 'I've been raped'. Nobody noticed anything. Next morning, Mum did say, 'You're looking peaky, love.' But I said straight off, 'I'm all right. Just a bit tired.' Mum and Dad had been chatting about the shop, as usual, how they'd got back early on account of things being slow. 'Things'll pick up later,' said Dad. 'Always slow after Christmas.' I could hardly take in just how normal he was being, and Mum too.

And that's how it went on. They didn't know, mustn't know. If I tidied it all away, it'd be as if it had never happened. But at the same time, I knew I was kidding myself. I couldn't pretend I wasn't shocked to my core by what Tarik had done.

Though I was asking myself, What had he done, really?

Yes, I knew it was rape. I'd heard the word, knew what it meant – or thought I did. A guy had sex with a girl when she didn't want it. And I didn't want it. Tarik must have known that, mustn't he? I was screaming. I was terrified. He must have known I was right upset. But was it really rape?

I think of myself then, not yet fourteen, and remember the confusion I felt. I'd had no sexual experience at all, hadn't even felt a sexual urge. I was like a kid, in that way. I even found myself wondering if this was actually what people meant by sex, this was what they did. I knew it was supposed to be something you liked, folk made such a fuss about it. Did Tarik have sex with me because he fancied me and that was his way of doing it?

But then I remembered the laughing. He'd laughed, and his mates had laughed, and it wasn't friendly, it was hurtful. They were laughing at me, not with me. That couldn't be right. And another thing – those flashes of light.

Afterwards, I didn't say much to Joanne about what happened, but I did ask about the flashes.

'Them flashes – they had cameras, didn't they?'

She looked down, shuffled her feet a bit. 'Yeah.'

'So they took photos of me,' I said.

'Yeah.'

Oh God. It was bad enough being exposed in the first place, they saw me with just about nothing on, but to think they'd taken pictures... My insides went cold. What would they do with the photos? Would they show them to everybody they knew – who knew me? That was right cruel.

There was one other thing I had to ask Joanne before we closed up on the subject.

'They made you look, didn't they?' I said.

She looked away. 'Yeah.'

We were quiet.

'I'm that sorry,' Joanne said after a bit. 'I couldn't stop him.'

''Course you couldn't,' I said, straight off. I wasn't blaming her. Even big Joanne was no match for that man.

So – the laughing, taking no notice of me, the

photos, making Joanne look. That must add up to something bad, mustn't it?

But I was in such a muddle, I didn't know what to think. I just couldn't get my head round it. Tarik had said something about us meeting again. He wanted to have sex again?

I could cry when I think of that young girl. So sure of herself, so cocky, so proud of her fancy friend. She had no idea what she was getting herself into – and if anybody had tried to tell her, if they'd known, she wouldn't have believed them, would've told them where to get off. She knew what she was doing. She knew that Tarik was her friend, he looked out for her, he was a great guy.

So he had sex with her. It was awful for her. Her world crashed down in a thousand pieces. He'd led her on, made her think he was something he wasn't. He'd hurt her, hurt her in more ways than one. But friends don't hurt you, not like this.

And yet...

What made her go back to him?

14

Rubbing It In

What else could I do? That's what I asked myself at the end of school that day. I'd somehow managed to keep myself going, pushing last night to the back of my mind and forcing it to stay there. It was kind of like when our dog Molly died years ago. I tried hard then not to let my feelings show, despite how upset I was, and I don't think anyone noticed anything odd about me this time. Like I said, I was different on the inside, in my head, the way I felt, not the way I looked.

I didn't dare say anything to Chloe. She'd been right about Tarik all along. You couldn't trust him. So when I bumped into her at school I couldn't let on what happened, just managed the usual 'Hiya!' with a smile on my face and the usual chat.

And it wasn't just Chloe. While I was sat at my desk, I think it was English, it suddenly flashed into my mind what Sophie had said that time – about

Joanne and young girls, and Asian lads...not Tarik by name, but she obviously knew something was iffy. And as for Claire – well, she'd made warning noises even sooner than Sophie and Chloe. How come they could all see it and I couldn't? I just couldn't get my head round it. What I did know was that I could never mention it to them. There was only Joanne who was in on it. She didn't say anything out of the ordinary during the day, but as we were packing up to go home, she asked me, 'Gonna go out tonight?'

I stopped stuffing my school bag, and looked at her. I was thinking, What! How can she think I'd go out after what happened? As I stood staring at her, she said, 'I mean, you gonna stay in now, or what?'

And that made me think. Did I want to stay in? What would I do? Sit at home and watch telly? Smoke a crafty fag in the back garden so Dad wouldn't smell it? Pinch some of his booze? And as for sneaking in some dope...

I felt my heart sinking. Boring, or what? I realised that over the past months I'd got used to going out in the evening, hanging out with my mates, having the best time. Did I really want to sit at home by myself?

No, I didn't. Then again, how could I go out to the usual places if Tarik might be there? And those other guys, who'd laughed at me and taken photos? My blood ran cold, and my throat closed up. But I wouldn't let those scenes play again in my head, I wouldn't. And I was feeling a spark of something else. If I hid at home, scared to go out, that would be one up to Tarik. He'd know he'd got to me, he'd have won. He might have raped me, but I'd go on being his victim, over and over.

I realised I was straightening up, looking Joanne in the eye.

'Yeah, I wanna go out,' I said. 'I'll be down road at half four. Okay?'

Joanne smiled, a wide smile. 'Good for you,' she said.

So after getting changed at home, I set out down the road to Joanne's, walking fast, head held high. This was the way to handle it, I thought. Push it away, don't dwell on it, and face it out. He couldn't hurt me again if I didn't let him. If I met him, he'd realise he might have got at my body, but he couldn't mess with my mind.

How wrong can you be?

As it happened, me and Joanne didn't see Tarik that evening in town. I was keeping an eye out for those other two, Azad and Imran, as well, but no sign of them either. We ran into some of the guys we hung out with, and they were friendly as usual. As far as I could tell, they weren't any different from usual, no looking sideways at me, no funny remarks. All in all, a pretty mellow evening. Good. Things can get back to normal.

The same went for the rest of the week. Maybe Tarik was lying low after what he did to me. Maybe he was worried that I'd make a fuss, go to the police. I didn't think it then, but later I wondered how he could be so sure that I wouldn't report him. There'd be plenty of evidence, all that forensic stuff you see on telly. But it honestly didn't cross my mind. And he must have known that. He knew me better than I knew myself. And it wasn't long before he proved it.

It was early the next week. Me and Joanne were hanging out by the war memorial, smoking, chatting, all laid back, with some of the lads. One of them was talking to me when he suddenly went quiet, looking over my shoulder. I knew it. It must be Tarik. I set my face, and turned round, casual like, and sure enough it was him. Well, it had to happen some time, and now was as good a time as any.

I looked him in the face, said, 'Hi.' Very cool.

Tarik smiled. 'Hi to you, Emma,' he said. 'I was hoping I'd run into you. I wanted a word. Let's go for a walk.'

And he took my arm, not hard, and steered me down to the back of the garden and the broken bit of fence. I found myself walking beside him like I'd done so many times before. It was like I was on automatic. But my mind was racing. What did he want? What was he going to say? He wasn't being angry, or hostile. He just seemed quiet and friendly, like the old Tarik. My heart suddenly leapt – maybe he was going to say sorry. He'd been out of his head on smack or something and didn't know what he was doing. He was really, really sorry. What would I say? I couldn't think. Could we get back to how we used to be?

By now we were in the alley and walking towards the end. Tarik turned me towards him, and looked me straight in the eyes.

Those eyes. I don't believe people can have evil eyes, they're only bits of the body, like your ears or your mouth. But there was something about Tarik's eyes. I found myself staring back at him. If I'd wanted to say anything I couldn't have.

Now he was talking softly. Softly, but the back of my neck was prickling.

'Emma, Emma, Emma,' he said, shaking his head. 'You really have to learn.'

Then suddenly he pushed me and I fell backwards. Then he was on me, and the nightmare was happening all over again. Scream for help! But he clamped one hand over my mouth. I could just about breathe through my nose, as I struggled and struggled. He was such a weight. He'd always seemed slightly built, but he was solid.

'The more you struggle, the more I like it,' he said, his face close to mine as he pushed himself into me. What? What could I do? The tearing pain again. It seemed to go on for ever, I thought I was blind as I could only see darkness. Then he was rolling off me, standing up, tidying his clothes. Like before, I got my own clothes back on as fast as I could.

I was crying and shaking. I wished the ground would swallow me up. As I sat there hunched up, I realised he was stroking my shoulder. 'Don't touch me!' I shuddered. He laughed, and took hold of my chin, squatting beside me. He forced me to look at him.

'Emma, there's something you have to understand. If I want something, I take it. Not that I want you all that much. To be honest, I fancy your friend Chloe. I've got a thing for red hair. Pity she won't hang around. But you'll do, for now.'

He held my chin tight, another pain.

'See?' he said. 'That's the way it is. I'll tell you what to do and you'll do it.' He put his face close to mine. 'Won't you?'

I just sat there, tears streaming down my face. If I'd felt shattered before, this was even worse. No mistake, he meant it.

Then he was sitting back on his heels, taking something out of his jacket pocket. It was a hankie, clean and white. 'Now wipe your eyes, and calm down,' he said. I was still shaking, so he dabbed at my eyes himself. He was gentle now, he even sounded kind. I had to shake my head to try and clear it. My mind was whirling, there was a pain in my stomach.

He helped me to my feet and straightened the collar of my coat, and smoothed my hair.

'Not like you to look untidy, Emma,' he said, and he made a tutting noise.

I stood there, as if I was frozen stiff. What had happened was still hammering in my mind. I didn't know what to do, what to think.

Tarik was talking again.

'Now,' he said, 'we are going back to join our friends. We've been for a nice walk, haven't we? And we're going to have a nice drink. Everything's nice, isn't it?'

He shook my arm. 'Isn't it?' he said again. And God help me, I found myself nodding.

'Good,' said Tarik. We turned to go back, then he held my arm again.

'Just to let you know,' he said. 'You won't go shooting your mouth off to anyone, will you? We don't want a fuss.' And he smiled as he moved his hands to my throat. Next minute, his fingers were digging into me behind my ears. The pain was sharp, and my eyes were swimming, I was blacking out. Then just as I thought I'd fall down, he stopped, and patted me on the shoulder. 'Useful, that,' he said, sounding very everyday, very matter of fact. 'Pressure points, you know. And the good thing is that the bruises don't show.'

He suddenly took hold of my shoulders and put his face very close to mine. The strong smell of his scent made my eyes water, and it was like I was crying again. His voice was hard.

'I can hurt you in all sorts of ways, ways that don't show. Cross me and you'll find out.'

Then he was back to being polite, taking my arm, and walking me back down the alley.

I walked like I was in a dream, one foot in front of the other. Now it was all ordinary again, sitting on one of the old benches, Joanne passing me the usual bottle of Smirnoff. This time I glugged it. It'd warm me up and make my head go woozy. The more the better. That would soften the edges of what happened. Likewise the joints. I had a couple, breathing the smoke in as far as I could, making everything go blurry.

I heard Joanne saying, 'Watch it, Emma, you're not Chloe, you know. I'm not carrying you home.'

Chloe. He said he fancied her. He couldn't have her so he'd have me. He didn't even like me, I was just handy. I didn't think I could feel any worse, but I did.

They do a good job, booze and dope. As far as I was concerned, they had to.

15

Shit on His Shoe

So that's how it went on. Not every day, maybe two or three times a week, for a month or so. 'Let's go for a walk,' he'd say, wherever we happened to be. That got to be almost like a catchphrase off the telly, only not funny. We'd be by the war memorial, or the yard we called the club, or the mall after closing, once or twice in the park outside town. One minute we'd all be hanging out, a whole group of us, next minute Tarik's taken my arm and off we'd go. Then we'd come back, and it was like we hadn't been away. Nobody said anything, or made rude jokes. It got to be kind of normal. I could almost believe that nothing had happened, if it wasn't for the pain inside my body and the hurt in my heart. They never got any less.

I tried to figure out just why Tarik was doing this to me. I might not have known much about sex, but I did know it was supposed to be something folk did when they liked someone, when they were attracted to them. I mean, you don't just pick someone up in the street, whatever they're like, and say, 'Right, let's go in bedroom.' There has to be a reason, I thought. The way he treated me, I couldn't believe Tarik even liked me, and I knew he fancied Chloe and not me, so why did he keep having sex with me? Or forcing it on me, I should say, as it was rape, no question. He must have known how much I hated it.

I knew he came inside me, and that was what men liked, I suppose, getting their end away. But I couldn't kid myself he was ever overcome with passion, couldn't help himself, like what happens in love scenes in movies. In fact, though I didn't have anything to compare it with, he seemed almost automatic, mechanical. Now and then he'd say something rude, like, 'I shaved my balls this morning – gonna lick 'em?' Which I thought was disgusting, but I don't think he expected me to say anything back. It was just something nasty, to put me in my place. And while I'm on the subject, he never forced me to do oral sex on him. It was in, bang, out.

One time, I had a crazy thought. I had a picture in my mind of him standing there with a clipboard and a timetable and a stopwatch. Tuesday, 7.30 p.m.: rape Emma. It almost made me laugh. But as it happens, I was nearer the truth than I could ever have known. After all, Tarik was nothing if he wasn't a businessman. He'd told me about strategy, how you need it in business. A plan. A goal. Taking the long-term view. And what he did to me was part of his strategy.

At the time, I found it all so confusing. Even the fuss he made about me not lying on bare concrete, if we weren't in the park where it was grass. Why should he care? The first time he'd raped me, the concrete ground was that rough my skin was scratched and torn to bits. Now, he told me to put my coat down on the ground first, to give me something to lie on. My coat, not his. What was that all about? Did he care, but just a bit? Not enough to put his own coat on the ground?

If I could've put two and two together then, I would've thought of something my dad had said, talking about finances. Protecting your investment.

Whatever, all this makes me sound like a right wimp. So much for standing up to Tarik, showing him what's what. He did what he wanted, and I just lay there and took it. All I can say is that I wasn't even fourteen yet, and nothing in my life had set me up for dealing with this, with a man like him. Of course I was scared of him – I knew he'd hurt me in more ways than one at the drop of a hat. And not just me.

One time he said, 'I'd hate us to fall out, Emma. I don't know what I'd do, I really don't. I'd be so upset. It'd make me feel like paying a visit to your mum and dad's shop. Busy place, isn't it? There they are, your mum and dad, working their socks off cos they'd rather be there than at home with you.' He shook his head. 'If I was very upset with you,' he went on, 'I might just throw something in the shop. Petrol bomb, maybe. What d'you think? Give your old nan a shock too, wouldn't it?'

I thought he'd do it. I thought he'd do anything. Though I couldn't remember ever telling him that my nan lived in the flat over the shop.

While I'm thinking about Tarik and the effect he had on me, a memory comes to mind. It was years ago, when Dad had taken me and Stevie for a day out in Scarborough. We'd had a lovely time, and we didn't want to leave, so it was late when we set off back home, really dark. Dad was just driving along, me and Stevie half asleep in the back, when he suddenly slammed on the brakes and we jolted forward.

'What's going on?' we asked.

'Look at it,' said Dad. 'Poor little bugger.'

Me and Stevie craned our necks to look through the windscreen. The car's lights were streaming ahead, and in them we saw a small shape.

'It's a rabbit!' said Stevie. 'Why's it just sat there, Dad? Why won't it move?'

'It's petrified,' said Dad. 'Scared stiff. Probably hasn't been out and about much – it won't know what light is. When rabbits are scared they just sit still. Hope danger goes away.'

I looked at the rabbit, its eyes huge and dazzled. I felt right sorry for it, one little rabbit in front of a great big car on a dark and lonely road.

'What're you gonna do, Dad?' I asked.

'Run it over,' said Stevie.

'No!' Dad shot back. 'We'll give it a chance. Road's quiet, nowt's about, so I'll turn off lights.'

We sat there in the dark, Dad looking all around to make sure another car wasn't in sight. A few minutes later he put the lights on low.

'It's gone,' he said. 'I knew it.' He started up the car and we were off again.

I just thought he was really kind. I bet a lot of drivers wouldn't spare the time and would've just run the poor thing over. I was proud of my dad for that.

Okay, I'm not a rabbit. But I could have done with someone, or something, turning off the light.

*

It's amazing what you can get used to. It was like a new way of life. And I found ways to deal with it. Not just the booze and dope, though they did help, after Tarik had done with me. I tried to sort it out in my mind. It may sound strange, but I thought of the dentist.

Not that I'd needed a dentist, I've got good teeth. It was Stevie. A while back he needed some fillings, not a surprise with all the sweeties he stuffed his face with. But the fuss he was making, you'd think his head was going to be chopped off. I remember Mum saying to him, 'Well, love, it won't be nice, but it won't last long. Just think of summat good you'll be doing after. That'll take your mind off it.'

So I tried that too. I'd lay there while Tarik was banging away and fix my mind on a good thing. Usually the booze and dope, and getting a good vibe going. It sort of helped, it did take some of my mind off it.

It couldn't disguise the look on Tarik's face, though, when he'd got off me. Like one big sneer, he thought that little of me. The nasty things he'd say, making me feel like a worm. Or shit on his shoe, that's what I am, I thought. Shit on his shoe. I was starting to hate myself, this person I'd become. I didn't realise at first what I was feeling. I'd never had cause to think of myself that way. Just taken myself for granted, you might say. But now I knew I was just shit, a worthless person. What can you do with a worthless person but hate her? She's not fit to live.

Then there was a reason to hate myself even more.

It was one evening, we'd got together in the garden behind the war memorial. Tarik wasn't there at first, and I was that relieved, started to relax.

Then he was at my shoulder, like out of the blue.

'Emma,' he said. 'I want you to meet someone.'

I looked at him. What was going on?

'He's a cousin of mine, come all the way from Bradford, so you mind you're nice to him.' He gripped my arm hard and put his lips close to my ear. 'Whatever he wants, you give it to him. Got that?'

Before I had time to think anything, he was marching me towards a man who must have arrived with him, as I hadn't seen him before.

'Azim,' he said, 'this is Emma. Emma, this is Azim.'

This Azim wasn't much to look at. He was old and fat, with little piggy eyes. His face was dark-skinned, darker than Tarik's, and was all sweaty. He was smiling at me. 'Hello, Emma,' he said. 'Pleased to meet you.' Then his smile got wider and he said, 'Let's go for a walk.'

16

Paki Shagger

I knew what they were calling me behind my back. I could hear the giggles and see the nudges. In the classroom when the teacher's back was turned, or in the dinner queue. Emma the Paki shagger. Though come to think of it, it should have been the other way round. It was them shagging me, not me shagging them.

I don't know how word had got around. I'd always thought our group in town was sort of exclusive – which was one of the reasons I liked being in it so much. But I suppose things get out, and folk can't resist a gossip. A chance to snigger and point the finger. As far as I was concerned, they could say what they liked. I didn't care. What did they know? Stupid kids. I wasn't going to be put down by them. I didn't want anything to do with them – or anyone else, for that matter. They could go fuck themselves. Except Joanne. She stuck by me, sat with me at dinner, went out with me most evenings.

We never talked about what was going on, me and Joanne. There was just that first time, when she'd said it was best to say nowt, pretend it didn't happen. It was sort of working, I supposed. I was meeting Tarik in town nearly every evening now – he'd text me after school and tell me where to go. He usually had a friend who he said wanted to meet me. Then it was off for a walk, round the corner or in the bushes, or in someone's car.

If I stopped to think about it, I felt like the bottom was falling out of my world, it was so horrible. Those men...I reckon they weren't Tarik's cousins or his mates at all. They weren't in his league. They were too old. All Asians, though, so I expect they all knew each other.

It was better not to think about it. Put up with them groping me, pulling my clothes down, raping me. Though when it came to getting clothes off, Tarik gave me a tip.

'Just take one leg out,' he said. 'Saves time. They can get stuck in quick as they like, and you don't have to faff about afterwards looking for your shoes and stuff.'

Tricks of the trade, I suppose. Just take one shoe off, one leg out of jeans and knickers, and off you go. The good thing about it as far as I was concerned was that I could get dressed afterwards much more quickly. No jeans and underwear flung about. That was always important to me – to cover myself up as soon as possible. When I was dressed again, that bad time was over.

I realise I've just said 'trade', but the funny thing is, I had no idea at the time what kind of trade I was in. Of course, I was a prostitute. I might not fit that old idea I had of what a pro looks like – all short skirt and low-neck blouse and fishnet tights, hanging about on street corners. I was a young girl in jeans and jumper and trainers. But that's what I was. And Tarik was my pimp. If he's selling my body, that's what it is. But for a long time that didn't hit home. I really thought I was just putting up with his so-called mates, like he was doing them a favour. It's not like he came straight out with it and said, 'Right, how many punters are you gonna do today?' Meaning, 'How much money are you gonna earn for me?'

These guys didn't usually hurt me like Tarik did the first time, at least, not so much. It wasn't so shocking now – I knew what to expect. It was still disgusting, though. A few of them tried to kiss me, but I wasn't having that. I always turned my head away. They could do what they liked with the rest of me, but as far as I was concerned, kissing was for when you liked someone. Kissing was sweet, and what these men were doing wasn't sweet.

Tarik had laid it on the line when he said I had to do what he wanted. When I came back crying that first time, with Azim, Tarik grabbed me by the arm and pulled me down the alley again, away from everyone.

'Look,' he hissed in my face. 'No crying. What d'you think you're doing? You're here to give that guy a good time, and don't you forget it. He's not gonna think he's got a good deal if you play up, is he?'

Deal? I was part of a deal?

He must have seen how I couldn't get my head round this, on top of everything else, as he spelled it out.

'They want a nice little girl, a nice little blue-eyed blonde. Remind you of anyone?' He twisted my arm. 'That's what they want and they pay good money for what they want. So that's what they're gonna get. You forget that, Emma, and you'll wish you'd never been born.'

So I didn't forget it.

There was one time, though, a month or so after all this started, where I couldn't help myself. I couldn't do it. I'd been for one of those walks with a man called Jav – another nickname, like the others. I never knew their real names. He was horrible, said filthy things, and he did hurt me. He even bit me. I was dead upset, couldn't have been more glad when it was over. Well, about a week later, Tarik's leading me over to a man, round the loading bay in the mall, and it's this Jav again. Even with Tarik there, I couldn't do it. I pulled myself away from Tarik, and made a run for it.

I was desperate to reach the bus station, but no chance. Tarik soon caught up with me, and when I saw his face, I could have died. It was all twisted, his eyes were glaring. He flung me face first against a wall, and jabbed me in the back with his fists. It was agony, I couldn't breathe. Then he dragged me up and pulled me round a corner, into one of the bays. He put his face right up to mine and spat at me.

'You disrespect me up like that in front of my friend – I'll kill you, you little bitch!'

And he grabbed hold of my hair with one hand and slapped me round the face with the other, again and again. I felt myself going limp, like a rag doll. Then he pushed me face down on the ground, yanked down my clothes, and was on me. But it was different this time, he was grabbing my bum, pulling me apart. Then I felt the most awful tearing pain, worse than anything I'd felt before, and he pushed himself into me, again and again. I thought I'd split in half. This was too much. I really thought, This is it. I'm gonna die. By now, I wanted to.

When he'd finished, he pushed his face close to mine again. With one part of my mind I saw what he was looking like – his eyes wild, dribble round his mouth. The rest of my mind was somewhere else.

He spoke to me, jabbing me in the chest with his finger. 'You do that again and I will rip you apart. Then I'll get hold of your mother and I'll rip her apart, then all my mates will rip both of you apart. Got that?'

I got it.

I don't know what happened to Jav that night. I just lay there on the cold ground for quite a while, crying and shaking. I was that despairing I thought I might as well never get up. Just stay there and freeze to death. But I guess I wasn't ready to die yet. I managed to pull myself together, tidy myself up, and walk to the bus station. I don't know how, though. My bum was so painful. I could feel blood dribbling out. I'd have to have a right good soak in the bath when I got home.

That was the pits for me. Nightmare. That was when something went really wrong in my head. At least, that's how I see it now. Tarik had forced me to have sex with him, and that was bad. Then with his so-called mates, and that was bad. But Jav was cruel, and Tarik's revenge…I couldn't take it. It made me feel at an all-time low. I'd known I was shit on his shoe. Now he was wiping me off it, I was that disgusting. It was as if something in my mind, or my heart, went cold and hard. Later, I realised I was building a wall between me and what was happening, just to survive. But then, it was like I was becoming another person, a person who could hardly think for herself when Tarik was around. A robot.

I met him a couple of nights later – he'd texted me with time and place as usual, my orders. Why did I go? Why didn't I tell someone, call the police? If you'd asked me that then, I would have just said, 'I can't,' without knowing why I couldn't. It wasn't just that I was so scared of Tarik, and believe me, I was scared of him. The thought he'd hurt my mum as well as me… And he'd already threatened to fire-bomb the shop. I couldn't bear to think of it. My family, all the people I loved, in danger because of me. I was that confused, my head was all over the place. I think I was waiting for someone to come up to me and ask me straight out, 'What's wrong, Emma?' Maybe that would've broken the spell, or whatever it was. But nobody did.

17

Hitting Out

I must say, though, if somebody had come up to me, all concern, and asked me what was wrong, I probably would've told them to eff off. I was getting sharper and sharper with everyone, real prickly. The smallest thing said to me and I was off on one. Even at school, where I'd been careful to keep up appearances. Now I didn't care. From being a model student I went to being on report most of the time. That's when you have to carry a bit of paper around with you and each teacher makes a comment on your behaviour in class. There were a lot of kids like that in my school, you'd see them walking round between lessons clutching their bit of paper. My A grades went to D and E.

And I didn't put up with teachers any more. No more nice little Emma – yes, sir, no, sir, three bags full, sir. If they said anything out of order to me, I let them have it right back. I can see the surprise on their faces now as I snapped at them.

I remember one lesson, it was IT, and we had a supply teacher. A right nerd. We were sat in twos at our computers and he told us to design a classroom. Well, me and Joanne weren't having it. We took it on ourselves to design a shopping mall – that was more like it, more our kind of thing.

'What are you doing?' he said when he stopped by us. 'That doesn't look like a classroom.'

'That's cos it in't,' I said, bold as you like. And me and Joanne burst out laughing. The teacher was really annoyed.

'Well, you can just start again,' he said, 'and do what I told you.'

'Don't think so,' I said, laughing more than ever. The look on his face! I found it was funny to see him at a loss for words. What could he do? He sloped off and me and Joanne went on doing our version of a shopping mall. Then he came round again and blew up.

'You're deliberately ignoring what I said.' He was red in the face. 'You can just go outside, the pair of you…blah blah blah.'

'Fine by me,' I said, and me and Joanne strolled out. When we got through the door I popped my head back in and said, 'We're off to get some pop and choccie from vending machine – want anything?'

'Get out!' he roared.

I really liked winding him up. I liked hurting him, I guess. He was just trying to do his job, and I wanted to mess it up for him. Making him feel bad made me feel better.

I didn't work it out at the time, I couldn't have, but I know now that a good way to hide your own hurt is to take it out on other people. That way, nobody knows you're worried and upset, they're just taken in by your attitude. You keep them at a distance, and that makes you safe, in a way.

So I was nasty to folk, and not just to teachers. It makes me ashamed now, but one day me and Joanne picked on a boy called Paul in our class. He was a boff – our name for a swot – and he was an easy target, small and weedy, always dressed in the proper uniform, which most of us weren't. One break time, we walked over to him and said, 'What's your problem?'

He hadn't been doing anything, was just sitting there minding his own business. We wanted to pick a fight. Well, we ended up grabbing his clean and tidy pencil case and chucking it all out the window, laughing at him as he couldn't stop crying. As bad things go, this wasn't exactly cutting his throat, I know, but I upset him, and that was what I wanted.

I liked it that people took a step back from me, that I'd gone from being sweet and friendly to hard and aggressive. I might be a Paki shagger, but I got some of the power that Tarik had, and swaggered about, just like him. It was like I grew another skin, a hard shell.

In fact, now I think about it, I was turning into a kind of Tarik, a younger, smaller, girl version. When the glamour had worn off him, I noticed that he wasn't the smooth-talking charmer I'd taken him for. He often said spiteful things, he had a cruel tongue. One of his mates, Bobby, had awful acne, his face was pitted with spots and scars. Tarik used to call him Pizza Face, and laugh, as if it was a joke, but I don't think it was. Bobby was very self-conscious about his skin, and Tarik seemed to take a delight in drawing attention to it, making Bobby go red and make his face look worse than ever. It doesn't sound much, I know, but it was a sign of what Tarik did, putting people down, reminding them he was the boss.

And he was the boss. The respect I thought I'd seen in people's eyes was more like fear. I didn't know at first that he had two brothers, older than him, but then I'd heard whispers. They were hard guys, but Tarik was harder. They were up to all sorts, and if you crossed them, you were sorry. Didn't I know it! How could I have been so blind? Even those 'deliveries', when I thought I was just running errands for Tarik, took me in. Of course it was drugs, I worked that out before long, and they weren't just dope. Hard stuff, I heard, crack, heroin....

I remember one time, I was in a car, waiting for someone. I was going to hand over one of those deliveries. This guy – I never knew his name, and never saw him again – got in and pushed a package under the driver's seat. It was wrapped in plastic, and I could see through it. Bank notes – twenties, fifties, a big wad.

Without thinking, I said, 'What's that then?'

And this guy said, 'Just been to cash machine.' Very casual. I was lucky he didn't hit me on the head for being nosy.

Well, news to me that you can get that amount of cash from a hole in the wall. From the size of it – well, I don't know how much. Must have been thousands. Big money.

I realise now they were trading on the fact that I was young, and had no record, no conviction for anything. If the police had happened to pull me up when I was carrying the bundle, I would've said the drugs were mine. That's what I was told to say, or else. How could the police prove otherwise? And if it got to court, there was me, a first-time offender. I'm not up for the same sentence as a grown man, one with previous convictions. I never did get pulled up, though, and that's another thing that makes me think. What if I had? Could I have kept my mouth shut? Would everything have come out in the open that much sooner?

I suppose I ought to be glad that Tarik never tried to get me hooked on the hard stuff. Later on, I knew that was the usual way with girls in the sex business. It wasn't out of the goodness of his heart, though – he must have known that if I'd got hooked I wouldn't have been able to cover it up. As long as it was just dope and booze, no one would notice much.

As I've said before, I worked it out. Put up with the really crap stuff, with those men, do what Tarik said, and deliver the packages when he told me – get the bad stuff over, and then enjoy the good stuff. Wipe my eyes, fix my make-up, face the world again. Like before, I had to take my mind off what was happening by thinking of something nice later on. Get pissed and high with my mates, feeling close to one another, talking about anything and everything, like in a bubble of something. The nasty stuff outside.

That's how I survived. In a few short months I'd gone from good girl to bad girl, and at the time I hardly even realised it. To this day I don't know how my parents didn't realise something was up – something really bad, I mean, out of the ordinary. I don't think the school ever got in touch with them, about the way my behaviour had changed for the worse. Not that I was holding back at home, either.

'You're doing my head in!' I'd yell at them if they even tried to talk to me. I can still see my dad's big face, all creased up with worry, shocked at the way I was carrying on. I'm sure Mum was still thinking it was adolescent stuff, hormones, that kind of thing, and she was all for being patient and sympathetic. But I didn't give her a chance, just yelled and slammed doors. Refused point blank to work in the shop on Fridays – 'I'm not your slave!' I wouldn't even take our dog out for a walk. We had another spaniel by now, called Maggie. Dad had brought her home one day, a tiny puppy, an adorable bundle of fluff, and we all fell in love with her. But now I just used her as another way of getting at Mum and Dad. 'You take her out! Get out of your precious shop for once!' Such screaming matches, I remember. I wouldn't let pass a single thing they said.

It was a way of letting the anger out, I suppose. And I was angry, not just mardy but spitting mad inside.

Stevie was right. I heard him one day, when he'd come home for another break. Just like I'd overheard him before, giving an honest opinion, he said to Mum and Dad in the kitchen, 'Well, I don't know. I never thought I'd say owt like it, but our Emma's turning into a right bitch.'

I hated myself, I hated everybody else, I couldn't see a way out. I was trapped for ever.

18

A Little Worm Turns

'No. I won't.'
'What? What did you say?'
'You heard. I said no I won't. I'm not going.'

I wouldn't have believed it. That was me, saying no to Tarik, straight out, to his face. What was that all about? How did I get from feeling trapped, under his thumb, to just about telling him where to get off?

We were in Tarik's car. Jakko in the driving seat as usual, Zane next to him, me and Tarik in the back either side of Joanne. We'd been cruising round town, and Tarik had just told Jakko to make for the mall. At this time of the evening, just as the shops were shutting, I knew what that meant. There'd be some old guy wanting to go for a walk. I don't know exactly what happened, but all of a sudden it was like something clicked in my mind. I won't. I won't do it.

I felt a kind of thrill in my gut, standing up to Tarik. I'd been getting a bit stroppy – in fact more than a bit stroppy – with him recently, and the way I figured it out was like this. He'd done his worst, hadn't he? He'd hurt me, abused me, dragged me through the mud – real mud, a few times. He'd forced me to go with other men. All the time he showed his power over me.

That was it. Power. I'd finally realised what Tarik got off on. He didn't rape me for any sexual pleasure he might get – or, if he did get any, that was by the way. What rang his bell was proving he could control me, make me do anything he wanted. So cocky, giving me my orders. That look on his face, after he'd forced me to have sex...as if he was king of the castle and I was some kind of low life. I didn't realise it at the time, and it's a horrible thought, but when he raped me those first times, it must have been to get me used to it, sort of, before lining up other men. It's like breaking me in. Then rape me now and then to remind me who's boss. Get a girl when she's young... No wonder I had that picture of him in my mind with a clipboard and stopwatch. All very businesslike.

So when I started thinking, What have I got to lose? What else can he do? – and not jumping the second he said jump, he must have thought I was getting out of line. That's the only reason I can think of for what had happened just the week before.

*

'Get in.'

Tarik was yanking open the passenger door of a car that had just stopped at the kerb. I was surprised – he hadn't said anything about meeting up with anyone, and we'd just been walking along the street in town, late afternoon. I hesitated on the pavement, and Tarik pushed me into the car. 'Get in,' he practically spat at me. 'You're going for a ride.'

Next minute the car was driving off, and I tried to catch my breath. What was all this about? When I went with men in their cars they were always parked somewhere quiet. We didn't go any place else.

I had a quick look at the driver. Not a pretty sight. Older than the other Asian guys I'd met, maybe in his forties, very skinny. A scarred face, thin lips and black hair greased up into little spikes. Well, I thought, what's his game? Somehow I didn't think he was after sex.

We drove for a while, then we were turning in at the gate of the park, going some way in. The driver stopped the engine and turned to stare at me. His eyes looked odd, the pupils very small. Before I could think anything, he reached down under his seat and then he was holding something, a dark shape... It took me a moment to realise it was a gun. I'd never seen one in real life before. It looked heavy.

Next minute he's pushing the end of it against my head. 'I'm gonna count to three,' he said. His voice was harsh. 'Then I'm gonna blow your head off.'

I sat in my seat, shocked rigid. It's not happening, I thought. It's a dream, a nightmare. My heart was thudding like mad, I could hardly breathe. For all I felt I had nothing to live for, I so didn't want to die. I heard his voice echo in my head. 'One...two...' I squeezed my eyes shut, though tears still poured out. I found myself saying, 'I'm sorry, I'm sorry...' I didn't know what I was sorry for, I'd say sorry for anything if only this would stop.

'Three.'

Then a click. No bang.

The only sound was this man starting to laugh. He laughed and laughed, as he put the gun back under the seat, and turned on the engine. I was trembling all over. I can't remember the drive back to town, but before long the car was pulling up at the bus station. The moment it stopped I flung open the door and scrambled out. The driver was still laughing.

Well, if that was supposed to be a frightener, it worked at the time. I was terrified. When the shock died down, though, I felt different. I was angry, being put through that on top of everything else. Then I was thinking, How pathetic. Tarik thinks he can keep me in line with this sort of trick? Who's he kidding?

I saw Tarik the next evening. Nothing was said, but I looked at him with even more contempt. Maybe he recognised it, I hoped he did. Maybe that's why he changed tactics the next time he raped me, to show he was still in charge.

It was the last time he raped me, though of course I didn't know that then. We were in the park, and he'd led me along one of the paths. It was late afternoon, still light. There and then he pushed me down on the ground, totally in public. Usually we went somewhere quiet, but not this time. It was like he was boasting out loud, he could do what he wanted, where and when he wanted.

I was lying there while he was banging away, my head turned aside as usual, and through my tears – I always cried – I saw something I'll never forget. A young couple were walking towards us, pushing a buggy. The baby was wearing something with blue and white stripes. They were chatting together as they got nearer, then they caught sight of us. They stood stock still, just for a moment, their eyes wide and their mouths open. I could see them from here. Then they whirled round, pushing the buggy back the way they'd come, but this time hurrying along.

I don't know what they thought. I've no way of knowing. Were they just embarrassed at seeing a couple having it off on the grass, did they feel they were intruding? There was a young girl obviously in distress, but their reaction was to get the hell out of it. Tarik was laughing, he thought it was hilarious. 'Scared them off,' he said. He must have felt on top of the world. I didn't.

But in a way I'm grateful to that young couple. I couldn't have expected them to rush to my rescue, though it does surprise me what folk can shut their eyes to. It made something click in my mind, it was another piece of the jigsaw that was building up. A jigsaw of what made me finally stand up to Tarik.

I think the last straw, later that week, was the pregnancy test Tarik made me take, in one of the public toilets in town. It's funny that this should've had such an effect on me, seeing as how he wasn't actually hurting me, at least my body. It was more like I felt even more worthless than usual, like an animal in a zoo, a thing and not a person. And it had to be him checking the result, not me. I had to hand over the tube thing right after I'd finished weeing on it. He was waiting outside.

How much lower could I go? Maybe there wasn't any lower. Maybe the only way is up...

*

Back in the car that day, I put myself on the line.

'Stop, stop.' Tarik was snarling at Jakko. Jakko turned round, his eyes wide, he looked worried. Tarik of course looked furious, like he would chew the carpet.

'You'll do what I say,' he snapped. Then he smiled his wide smile, which once I'd thought was charming and now looked plain evil. 'Don't forget your birthday present is waiting for you!'

Oh yeah, he'd mentioned that. It was a few weeks before my fourteenth birthday, in the middle of May. He knew the date, like he knew a lot of things about me.

'I've got an idea for a present for you,' he'd announced.

Despite everything, I still had a quick feeling of interest, anything to do with birthdays. Still a kid, I suppose. I couldn't resist asking, 'What?'

He grinned. 'I'll line up every guy you've been with, and let them do you, one after another. You'll like that, won't you? Real birthday party. We can take photos.' And he laughed, but it wasn't an I'm-only-joking laugh.

My heart sank to the ground. Apart from anything else, I was always worried about the photos, the ones those men took when Tarik first raped me. I thought of them being shown around, me all exposed. Insult to injury.

But now the new, sassy Emma spoke up. I was almost enjoying myself, in a funny kind of way. 'Can't make me,' I said, putting a grin on my face. I nearly stuck my tongue out at him, like a rude little kid! I heard Joanne take a sharp breath, and she squeezed my arm. Then she tried to calm things down.

'Anyone want a fag?' she said, getting a packet out of her bag. She was opening the packet when Tarik snatched it from her, pulled out the fags and started pulling them to pieces, flinging the bits round the car.

Temper, temper, I thought. I probably smirked.

Tarik was really working himself up by now. He leaned over Joanne and punched me in the side of the head – bang! He was a bit awkward, so it didn't hurt as much as it might have. When he spat at me, 'I'll show you, you bitch,' I could still talk back.

'Show me what?' I said.

'I'll fucking kill you.' Then he punched the back of the driver's seat. 'Jakko, get me that crowbar, I'll smash her fucking face in.' I knew he kept a crowbar under the seat.

Then he changed tack. 'Jakko, you fucking great streak of piss, I can't move here.'

Jakko being so tall, he had to have the seat set right back. So Tarik went off on one, telling poor Jakko, 'I'm gonna chop your fucking legs off!'

I just looked at him, spit coming out of his mouth, eyes crossing. What are you like? I thought. He was getting off his head now. Come to think of it, I reckon he must have been on something to lose his rag so fast.

He was still going on about the crowbar, which Jakko kept under the seat. I decided it was time to make myself heard.

'D'you know what, Tarik?' I said, right loud. 'If you wanna smash my face in, go ahead. I'll get out of car and lie down in road and you can do what you like. Cos you know what you are? You're a pussy. Men that hit women are pussies, and you're the biggest pussy of 'em all. I'll make it easy for you.'

God, I don't know where the words came from. I just knew I wanted to hit him where it hurt. And it hurt – I thought he'd explode.

'Get out the fucking car and I'll kill you!' he screamed.

Just then, Jakko spoke up. He actually spoke up for once.

'Not here, Tarik,' he said through his teeth. 'Too many folk about.' Sure enough, crowds were milling about on the pavements on their way home from work and shopping.

'Think I care?' Tarik spat. But Jakko stuck to his guns.

'You can't do owt here,' he said. 'Let it go.'

He turned to me. 'Get out, Emma,' he told me. 'You too, Joanne. Quick.'

Joanne was leaning across me, opening the door, pushing me out. As she slammed it shut, Tarik yelled, 'I won't forget this, Emma. You'll be sorry!'

I just waved a hand, all casual. 'Yeah, whatever.'

'Come on, Emma,' said Joanne. 'Don't push it. Let's get out of here.' And still gripping my arm, she marched me down the street, towards the bus station. She made me walk so fast I didn't have the breath to say anything.

When we reached the bus stop, Joanne relaxed her hold, and we sat on the hard, cold plastic seats. The days were longer now, in mid-March, but the winter hadn't let go its grip yet.

Joanne turned to me. 'What the hell's got into you?' she asked, straight out. 'What d'you think you're doing, winding him up? You know what he's like.'

'Don't care,' was all I said, and Joanne sighed a big sigh.

'He'll get you,' she said, 'you know he will.'

'Don't care,' I said again.

'Oh, Emma, what's brought this on?'

This time I just shrugged, and Joanne shook her head. She seemed to be really upset for me. Though I couldn't help wondering if she was scared for herself.

When we got off the bus in the village, Joanne hurried me up the road again.

'Don't hang about,' she said. 'Best be safe indoors.'

19

Shit Hits the Fan

So I got myself safe indoors. Nobody in, of course, except Maggie. She'd started barking the minute I put my key in the door. I got a bit of cold pie from the fridge, though I didn't really feel like eating, and went up to my room. I curled up on my nice soft bed, and must have dozed off, as I woke up with a start when the phone rang downstairs. It rang and rang, so I thought I'd better answer it.

It was Mum.

'Emma, are you all right, love?' she asked. She sounded worried.

'Yeah,' I said, ''course I am. Why wouldn't I be?'

'Oh Emma,' said Mum, 'don't start. I just want to know you're all right.'

'Why?'

'Mary next door's just rung us at the shop. She says there's a car been driving up and down our road, with a couple of lads in it. Asian lads, she could see that from her window. They were staring up at our house. One of them got out and walked to front door, only he set dog barking and they drove off. What did they want?'

'How should I know?' I said, off-hand. As if I'd tell her!

'Well, you do know Asian lads, don't you?' she said.

'So what?' I shot back. 'If they wanna talk to me they can get me on me mobile, can't they?'

'What are they doing then?' asked Mum.

'How should I know?' I said again. 'Maybe they're lost.'

'Okay, Emma,' said Mum. 'I'll leave it there. I'll be back soon.'

Well, I thought, putting the phone down. Tarik didn't waste much time. Putting the frighteners on me, was he? What were they going to do – ring the door-bell and snatch me off the doorstep? I checked my mobile for messages. Sure enough, there was a text from Tarik: 'U R 4 it.' Oh very sophisticated, I don't think. I felt a rush of contempt for the man. I knew what he was capable of, but right then I really didn't care. I wouldn't think about the future.

When Mum and Dad came home, I made out I was asleep so they couldn't go on at me. Next morning, Mum tried to grill me about those Asian lads, but I wasn't having any of it.

'How the hell should I know?' I snapped. 'I told you, I don't know owt. Why're you always getting at me? I hate you!'

In all the fuss and grumbling, I forgot to pack my mobile in my school bag, and stomped off without it. Funny to think of it, but that one small thing made big things happen.

Mum was sitting at the kitchen table. She was very still, sort of drooping. This wasn't like my mum, a right ball of energy most of the time. She stared at me as I came in – straight from school, for once, as I needed my mobile to see what was happening, if anything.

And there it was, on the table in front of Mum. I'd never seen such a look on her face, it was like she was carved out of stone. Then she spoke, and her voice was very soft.

'Emma,' she said. 'Please come and sit down. I want to talk to you.'

My stomach felt like it flipped over, while my heart started thudding hard. I felt for a chair and sat down, staring at the floor. Neither of us spoke for a minute, then Mum said, 'Emma, I know something's wrong.'

Oh no, this was it. What I'd dreaded, it was happening.

'I were sure those lads were up to no good last night,' she said. 'And when you wouldn't talk, I thought I'd better try and find out. So I checked your phone.'

That made me lift my head, but before I could say anything, Mum went on. 'I wouldn't touch your things as a rule, Emma, you know that. I've always respected your privacy. I've always trusted you. But something's changed.'

I could only sit and wait.

'There were a lot of messages from someone called Tarik, so I tried ringing his number – Tarik is a he, in't he?'

I nodded.

'Well, I only got a recorded answer, so I tried another one. Jakko. I got through this time. When he said hi, thinking I was you, I told him. I said, "I'm Emma's mother." Well, you could have cut the silence with a knife, then all of a sudden he's talking nineteen to the dozen. "It weren't me," he said. "It weren't me. I never touched Emma, I never hurt her, I always looked out for her." He went on and on, then he said, "Look, it weren't me. It were Tarik. Ask Emma, she'll tell you." And he rang off.'

Mum looked at me, direct in the eyes. 'Well, Emma,' she said. 'Will you tell me?'

I felt myself shaking. I'd been dreading this moment, when it all came out, but now it was here... I found it hard to breathe, I was gasping, then it was like a flood coming over me. I was crying, crying, crying my heart out.

In a flash Mum was beside me, holding me tight, stroking my hair. 'Oh Emma,' I heard her say, her voice choking. 'Oh my love.' Then she was sobbing too.

I don't know how long it was till we cried ourselves out, got ourselves back together. Mum straightened up. 'I'll put kettle on,' she said.

With mugs of tea on the table, Mum said, 'Please tell me, Emma. I know you've been hurt, and it were this Tarik. What happened, love? You can tell me.'

So I did. I said the words I'd never spoken out loud.

'He raped me, Mum. He raped me.'

Mum was gripping her tea mug, and as her hands shook it slopped over. She's not wiping it up, I thought to myself. Usually she's on to spills like a shot.

She took deep breaths. 'You stay sat there, love. I'll call your dad. He has to know.'

It was like everything was out of my hands. I heard her phone in the front room. Her voice didn't sound right. Dad must have known something was wrong even before she said, 'Jason, Emma's been hurt. Get home quick. Joanie'll take over.' Then, 'No, not now.'

She came back to the table and hugged me. 'It's gonna be all right, Emma. It's gonna be all right.'

We sat there holding our mugs, then there was the sound of a car engine roaring in the road outside our house, and brakes screeching. Then thudding footsteps, a key in the door, and Dad burst into the kitchen.

He stood stock still in the doorway, his eyes wild, flashing at me and Mum in turn.

'What is it? What is it? Emma? Emma, what's wrong?'

Mum took a deep breath. 'You'd best sit down, Jason.'

I'll never forget the look on my dad's face. It was like he'd been hit with a thunderbolt, his world crashing down. Then my big, burly dad was kneeling beside me, holding me, saying my name over and over, his voice breaking, choked with tears. With him so close, I could feel his heart beating fast, so fast it could have jumped out of his chest.

Though it doesn't feel like it at the time, there's only so many tears you can cry, aren't there? At long last, all three of us got our breath back, wiped our faces, sat looking at each other.

Then the questions started, as I knew they must. When? Where? How?

I just shook my head, and Mum said, 'Oh, Emma, we only want to help, love.'

Dad was pacing the floor, smacking one fist into the other hand.

'Police,' he said. 'Call police. They've gotta catch this bastard. Yeah, catch him before I do!'

He stopped pacing and looked straight at me. His eyes were blazing blue. 'By God, Emma, before I do. If I get my hands on him I swear—'

Mum cut in. 'Jason,' she said, 'that won't help. I'll call 999. Take it a step at a time. We have to do what's best for our Emma. Police'll know what to do.'

That stopped Dad. 'Yeah,' he said with a big sigh. 'You're right. Best for our Emma.'

So things got under way. It took the police an hour or two to come round, a couple of constables. One was a woman – I suppose there'd have to be a woman when it's a rape. She was kind, sat with me at the kitchen table and said, 'Right, love, now tell me what happened. Take your time.'

Tell her? Tell her what? Everything? I couldn't cope with that – it was too huge. I'd stick to Tarik. I wouldn't tell them about the other men. What if they thought I was a prostitute, a common prostitute? I couldn't let Mum and Dad know all that. A rape was bad enough. I'd have to pick and choose what I said, make out it was just Tarik.

I started with his name, that was easy. 'He's called Tarik,' I said.

The nice policewoman suddenly sat up. She looked shocked, and she glanced over at the other cop. His eyebrows were raised, and he came over to us.

'Tarik,' he said. 'If it's who I think it is, that makes a difference. This is a job for the big boys.' Then he said to the policewoman, 'I'll go outside and call 'em, okay?'

She nodded, and stayed sat with me while he went out. She had an odd expression on her face, and squeezed my hand. My mind was racing. They knew who he was! There couldn't be another bad man with his name, could there?

But, I thought to myself, the name didn't mean much months ago when Joanne reported her mobile missing, told the police Tarik had nicked it. The desk sergeant couldn't have cared less. What's happened since?

I didn't get an answer then, or when the other policemen came later that night. I think they were a special kind of squad – anyway, they didn't wear uniforms.

So then it was more questions. At one point I went upstairs and dug out those dirty clothes, the ones I was wearing when Tarik first attacked me. They were still hidden in the drawer in my wardrobe. When my mum saw them, she put her hands over her face. 'Oh, Emma,' was all she said. Dad didn't say anything, just went out the back door into the garden. The police were pleased, though. 'Good girl,' they said. 'Hard evidence.' They packed the clothes away in plastic bags, and stuck labels on them.

You'll have seen the procedures on telly. Police, doctors, more police, more questions. All grinding on. I felt as much like a robot now as I did before, doing what I was told, going where I was told, but this time people were helping me. And it was over, I told myself. Over. It'll never happen again.

But it did.

20

Under the Carpet

'Maybe it's for the best, love,' said my mum. I knew both she and my dad were very worried about a court case. Even if I could give my evidence by video link, or whatever it is, they reckoned it would all be a huge trauma. Me, I didn't think anything could be worse than what had happened to me. Anything after that was a piece of cake in comparison.

I'd answered all the police questions as best I could, and I gave Joanne's name as a witness. They went off to do their thing, and meanwhile, I had to be checked out by doctors in hospital. I must say they were really good to me, very kind and gentle.

'You see, Emma,' the gynaecologist had said to me, 'we're not checking just to see if you've picked up infections, but whether there's any damage that could stop you having children later on.'

She'd been very frank. She was used to girls in my

situation, she told me. I hadn't realised just how wide-spread it was, this using and abusing young girls. Turns out there's more than one organised gang in this part of the country. She told me one story that made my hair stand on end. One day a girl had been rushed in, in a terrible state. She must have got out of line or something, as the men she was with had poured bleach into her, right inside her, and left her to die. Somehow she'd managed to phone for help, and the doctors had done all they could.

'But she'll never be the same,' my gynaecologist said. 'Her insides are burnt out. She'll never have children, in fact she probably won't even be able to have sex ever again.'

I was shocked rigid, went cold at the thought of it. That poor young girl, no older than me, her life ruined. Just think, I thought to myself, that could have happened to me. Rather than that, I'd slit my throat. Though it didn't seem like it at the time, I must have been lucky.

In fact I was very lucky altogether. For all the men who'd used me, and none of them had worn condoms, I hadn't caught any sexually transmitted disease, none at all. My gynaecologist was amazed, and very glad for me. The way I figured it out was like this. The men I went with were all Muslims, as far as I knew, and they were very careful about the girls they used, they'd have to be clean. If the men caught anything, they'd give it to their wives, wouldn't they? And those wives would have been brought from Pakistan or wherever, and were definitely virgins when they were married, so they wouldn't have picked anything up. If the men were sick, the wives would find out, and it'd be shaming.

Well, that's the way I see it. And my luck carried through, as I never fell pregnant either. Yes, it could have been worse.

The legal side of things didn't go so well, though. The police had picked up Tarik, and he denied everything. Said we'd had a relationship for a while, but with no sex, and I'd got pissed off with him over something, and was crying rape in revenge. I thought about the forensic evidence I had, those stained clothes, and thought that must put him in the frame. But before things went much further, I dropped all charges.

Why? In one word: intimidation. First off, Joanne took back her statement. When the police first talked to her, she'd backed me up. Then a week later she denied everything, said she'd been drunk or something and all confused. As far as she knew, Tarik would never have laid a finger on me, never have hurt a hair on my head. Then I got a call from Chloe, who I hadn't heard from for a while.

'You'd best call it off, Emma,' she said. 'I'm hearing of all sorts they'll do to you, and your mum and dad, if you go ahead.'

So they were leaning on Joanne and Chloe. Then there were silent phone calls, and big black cars with smoked glass windows cruising round the estate, even keeping pace with me as I walked to school.

I can do without this, I said to myself. And that's when Mum thought it was for the best to drop the charges. It's not that she and Dad wanted Tarik to get away with it, he deserved punishment and I deserved justice. But would Tarik going to prison make me feel any better? I didn't think so. In fact I didn't care what happened to him. He was as much shit to me as I was to him. With a big difference, though. I was going to put my life back together, I was going to do well. I saw myself catching up on my education, getting the GCSEs and A levels, then off to university and a good career. Somewhere along the line I'd fall in love with a great guy, we'd get married and live in a nice house. Then there'd be children, best of all.

Meanwhile, I knew what would happen to Tarik – I'd seen it happen to some of his older mates. He'd never change. He'd never really achieve anything in life. He'd got by on easy charm, money was easy come, easy go. But there was nothing solid about him. He'd stay where he was, in a ghetto, slipping down because he didn't have what it takes to lead a decent life. He was a pathetic criminal, and he wasn't going to have any more effect on me.

So, I thought, I've escaped unscathed, physically, and I've put Tarik in his place. I've got it sorted.

I couldn't have been more wrong.

Going back to school was one of the ways of getting back to a normal life, but Mum and Dad were worried about that. They went to the school and spoke to the head, said I'd had a terrible time and needed proper care, and what about security? They were imagining horrible men lying in wait for me at the school gate.

The head didn't have much to say, as it turned out. The only suggestion was that I'd go to a special unit, where all the kids with learning and behavioural diffi- culties were put together.

'But Emma's not got those difficulties,' my dad told the head. 'You're treating her like she's the one with the problem, and she's the victim here.'

No dice, though. What's more, my dad reckoned that from what the head said, the way he was uncom- fortable, this wasn't a new situation for one of his students to be in. Just like I'd heard at the hospital. My eyes were opening, all right. It seemed that the powers that be wanted everything kept quiet. Wouldn't warn kids of the dangers out there.

Cut a long story short, Mum and Dad suggested a new school for me, starting in the summer term. I wasn't bothered, me. I didn't have much energy, so just went along with it. It was their way of sweeping what had happened under the carpet, making out that whatever had happened was over, and life goes on. I don't mean that unkindly, about the carpet. I'm not suggesting for a minute that Mum and Dad wanted to hide anything. They'd been devastated when they found out, blamed themselves left, right and centre though I told them not to. I knew that whatever I'd decided to do, they would have been with me every step of the way. No, I was sweeping just as hard as they were.

We none of us had a clue. As we tried to get back to normal, life actually got very abnormal. For a start, Mum and Dad were nearly always around. From working all hours, they'd changed tack. They took on another regular part-timer in the shop, and worked shifts, so when I was home, there was always one of them with me. And they were so nice to me. Walking on eggshells, I realised later, desperate not to upset me, but it was all part of things not seeming real.

School wasn't much better. Don't get me wrong, it was fine as schools go, and all girls, which was a change. But I was a fish out of water. The girls were nice, I made sort of friends but no one I could call a true friend, a close friend, a real mate. By this time, everyone had formed their own groups and I was never going to be a proper part of one. Then again, the girls my age seemed so childish, going on about boy bands and all that kind of thing as if they really mattered. I'd look at them, and think, You're the same age as me, but really I'm a hundred years older than you.

I seemed to drift through life in a bubble. Mum or Dad drove me to school every morning and picked me up in the afternoon – not just for security, as there wasn't a bus from our village. Then there was no question of going out in the evenings, so it was just us three and my homework and the telly. At weekends, I never went out by myself, except to pop in on Nan and Auntie Sue.

Dad had told Auntie Sue about what happened, and she was another to blame herself. 'I should have noticed,' she said, over and over till I could have screamed. How could she have noticed? Whatever, we didn't have our old, easy, close relationship. Nan knew a bit, but Dad had toned it down for her. I don't think she really understood much of it, except that I'd been hurt. 'But you'll be all right now,' she said, holding my hands. I hoped so, but life really was very strange. No way was it normal. I'd mope about the house, desperate for a fag, or a spliff, or a stiff drink, wishing I was anywhere but here, even with the people who loved me most and wanted to protect me.

It was the summer holidays when I finally cracked. Gave in, I mean, to myself. With no school, there'd be hours when I was on my own. I felt I was climbing the walls. There was no seeing Joanne, Mum and Dad were dead set against that, and I couldn't blame them. I never knew the real truth about Joanne's part in everything. As time went by, I found myself not caring. She was a friend once and now she wasn't. I didn't see her again. After a few phone calls Chloe had drifted away. Well, she had her life, good luck to her. She was all right, was Chloe.

I did think of another friend, though, one of the gang we'd knocked around with. So I phoned him.

21

It'll Be Different This Time

I'd known Ahmed since before Tarik. He'd always been nice, never tried anything on. He'd been sending me the odd text saying he was thinking of me, which was kind of him. After I rang him, we'd talk a lot on the phone, about anything and everything. I remember one evening, we were both sat in our houses watching *EastEnders*, and talking to each other about it all the way through! 'Don't like the look of him...' 'What an idiot...' Daft things you do with your mates. After a few chats I thought I could tell him how I was feeling, how I was sick of four walls.

Well, he had a good idea right off, said just the right thing to cheer me up. 'I'll pick you up in the village. We'll go to town. Like the old days.' Then he checked himself. 'I mean the good times,' he added.

And it was great. Sinking into his car, knowing I'd have a drink and a smoke, all the chat. I don't think I stopped smiling all morning. I thought I'd better get back early afternoon, before Mum got home. I knew she wouldn't understand. I could hear her in my head. 'What d'you mean, you've gone out with those lads again? Haven't you learned your lesson?' Of course, she didn't know Ahmed was nothing like Tarik.

So I kept it quiet, just fitted in the odd trip. It was on one of these that Ahmed introduced me to a couple of his mates, Abdul and Shabba. They were fine, everything was great. Then one day there was a new man in the group, and I took against him right away. 'Straight off the boat,' Ahmed said, grinning, and sure enough, this man was dressed in traditional clothes, a baggy top and trousers, white but none too clean. He had a big beard, all bushy, and truth to tell he looked like a tramp, a dirty tramp. What on earth were these smart young guys doing knocking around with him? I'd heard them say often enough what they thought of recent immigrants to this country, at least those who stuck to the old ways. They had a name for such people, which sounded like *manga*. They used it for people they thought were lowest of the low.

I never did know this new man's name. I certainly couldn't understand anything he said, mumbling through broken, black teeth. I just thought of him as the *manga*. At least I found out what his attraction was – 'He's house-sitting,' explained Ahmed. Apparently his whole family had gone back to the old country for a long stay, and he was the one left to look after the house. My friends all lived at home with their parents still, so it'd be handy for them having somewhere private to go to. I couldn't think of any other reason they'd put up with him. I tried to keep my distance, the few times I was in his company. I don't know if I was picking up on what they thought of him, but he gave me the creeps. I just tried to concentrate on enjoying myself.

A couple of weeks later, Ahmed picked me up from the village as usual, Abdul and Shabba along with him, and said, 'Fancy a drive in town, Emma?' Fine by me, so we went on what turned out to be a magical mystery tour through the streets. It was like a maze. I started to feel a bit uneasy, and thought I'd better try and work out where we were going. We seemed to be doubling back on ourselves half the time.

I'm not sure what was going through my head, but I started looking for landmarks, so I could keep some kind of track. A cinema here, a café there. At one point, Ahmed stopped outside a pub and popped in for a bottle. I tried craning my neck to see the name of the pub, but I was in the back, on the road side, and I couldn't see past Abdul. Still, I could see it had bright blue walls, which was unusual. And it turned out we were nearly there, where we were going, as Ahmed soon turned left and stopped outside an old house in a cul-de-sac.

'Here we are,' he said, and we all trooped up the front steps to the door. When it opened, I could have died. It was the *manga*, grinning away. This must be the house he was looking after.

Before I knew it, Ahmed was hustling me in, very cheerful, telling me to make myself comfortable. It was pretty run down, to be honest, but I found somewhere to sit, and soon had a drink and a smoke. I was wary, though, didn't feel like relaxing. A couple of other guys were lounging on a settee. I'd never seen them before, but everybody else seemed to know them, chatting away, all very friendly it seemed.

Then Ahmed stood up and said, 'Emma, would you mind coming in here a minute?' He opened a door and waved me in. The first thing I saw in this room was an old bed, a single bed with iron legs. Ahmed was smiling. 'Won't be long,' he said, smiling, as he stepped through the door and locked it from the other side.

Locked it. My legs just about gave way, and I found myself sitting on the floor, on a grubby, threadbare carpet. My heart was thudding, I could hardly breathe. Not again, I thought, not again. How could I have walked into this? How could I have fallen for it?

Because I knew what was coming.

The easy way, I thought, I must do it the easy way. Let them do what they want, get it over with, then I'll be out of here and home in time for my tea. I'll get clean, and curl up in my warm, safe bed. If I put up a fight, they'll beat me up, hurt me, and do what they want anyway. They might not even let me go. So grit your teeth, I told myself. Think about something else.

It just about worked, for a bit. They must have been deciding who'd go first, and it was Abdul. He wanted me to do some disgusting things, but I won't talk about them. Just get it over, just get it over. Then the two strange men, one after the other, then Shabba, then Ahmed.

Ahmed. Just like Tarik, a smiling face but an evil heart. I wasn't feeling like beating myself up over how stupid I'd been. That'd come later. But when he said, 'Just one more,' I realised who he meant.

'Not him,' I begged, 'not him.' The *manga*. Oh my God, with the guys I knew, if a *manga* touched a woman she was dead meat, lowest of the low. That was me. I pleaded and pleaded, but Ahmed turned on his heel.

'Gotta pay for the room,' he said.

Then the *manga* was on me, and in me, and I felt like I was in hell.

If I think coldly about it, he was no more violent or disgusting than most of the other men who'd done me. He was dirty and smelly, true, which was nasty, but it was more what he signified. I'm the lowest of the low. I hadn't thought I could get any lower, but here I was. With the Asian men, I knew how their circle worked. If they let a *manga* touch me, that's it – I'm not clean. It was as if they were saying, 'We've all used you, had our fun out of you, emptied our balls, and now you can just be anybody's. Anybody who can pay for you can have you.'

I'd hit rock bottom.

At first, I tried blocking it out. I got home safe enough – Ahmed drove me, chatting away as if he was talking about the weather, while I concentrated on the roads, desperate to make sure we were going home and I wasn't being taken away some place. Then I had a hot shower, tried to eat something.

I thought I knew how to deal with it. This total betrayal, for the second time. It kept hammering home to me. I was lowest of the low. They'd proved it.

So what should I do? It'd have to be business as

usual, sweeping everything under that carpet again. Believe hard enough and it'd be like it never happened. So don't talk about it, don't think about it, tell no one. Be even more on your guard and you'll get over it.

But I didn't.

22

Picking Up the Pieces

I tried to hold myself together, I really tried. I'd managed to hide everything before, when Tarik was around. But it was different this time. There was no looking forward to good times when the bad times were done with. Now, if this went on, it would be all bad times. And I swore to myself that I wouldn't let them happen again. Now I was dead meat, only fit for the dregs. If it was a choice between being touched by one of them, I'd cut my throat, I would.

At the time, I never stopped to think about just why I was feeling like this. As if it's worse to be raped by one man than another. I'd taken on their way of thinking, all right, my so-called friends. Judging myself by what they believed. At night, in bed, when it all washed over me and I thought my heart would break, I tried to cry quietly, so as not to let on to Mum and Dad. But Mum suspected something was up.

A few days later, I was sat with her in the conservatory, a bright summer morning, everything colourful in the garden. She'd made us a brew, and I was stirring my cup, round and round. That's what I remember, the sound of the spoon clinking on the cup. Something made me look up, and there was Mum sat staring at me, looking dead worried.

'You'll wear out that china,' she said.

I stopped stirring, and started to shake.

Well, it all came out, or most of it. I couldn't tell Mum about all those other men Tarik organised, not yet, but I talked about Ahmed. Mum knew what she needed to know, and she went into action. Police again, the doctor...and this time there was someone who talked to me a lot, a psychologist – or psychiatrist, I wasn't sure of the difference. There was another woman, too, a social worker apparently. I was getting the full monty this time. I worried a bit about the social worker. No one in our family had ever had anything to do with social services, and I thought Mum and Dad would think I was letting them down, that I was a bad girl, like you read about in the papers.

But of course Mum and Dad weren't having any of that.

'Whatever it takes to get you through this,' they said, more than once. 'We're with you all the way.'

I knew they couldn't understand why I'd gone back, and I didn't know how to put it into words. 'I was bored' might not seem enough of a reason, just make me look like a right lame brain, and of course there was more to it than that. I was trying to get back the good times, when I was close with my mates, we'd have a laugh, with just enough dope and drink to make everything even more of a buzz. I was so missing it all. That must be why I was such a dickhead, to fall for the old routine one more time. For God's sake, no one could have had more of a warning than me. Maybe I was still too young to learn that hard lesson, really learn it. If I was offering friendship, I still expected to get it back.

As I say, a dickhead.

Still, I had done one sensible thing, to make a note of that car ride round town. I remembered the pub with the blue walls, and pointed it out to the police when they drove me about the town. From there it was an easy step to the *manga*'s house, and later he was pulled in for questioning, along with Ahmed and his two mates. I never heard of the other two men, the strangers, ever again.

I wondered what would happen this time. Would we get the frighteners put on us again? Would we have to drop charges?

It was different this time. As far as I could gather, the men cooked up a story. One of them, Shabba, owned up to having sex with me, but said he thought I was seventeen. And me just a slip of a girl who didn't even look fourteen! The other men denied all knowledge.

My solicitor explained it. 'That man, Shabba, is the youngest, and he's got no previous convictions, clean as a whistle. So it'll look as if he has a good character. He'll try to persuade a jury that you said you were seventeen, and willing to have sex. These cases are always very tricky, one word against another.'

In the event, the case seemed to collapse. The CPS apparently turned it down.

I suppose I could have thought that was insult to injury, not to be taken seriously, not to be believed, but by then I didn't care. I was falling apart.

I don't remember much of the rest of that summer. I reckon I lost the plot for a while, I was really sick. Everything was catching up with me, and it was all I could do to get up in the morning and put one foot in front of the other, I was that exhausted.

I do remember my mum talking about this one day, when she'd come with me to the psychologist. 'Our Emma's real tired all the time,' she said. 'She can sit on settee all day, never lift a finger, and she's spark out by evening.'

She wasn't complaining, I know that. She was just

puzzled. She's such a bundle of energy herself she couldn't understand why I could look all right but be so dozy.

The psychologist explained it. 'Emma might not be doing anything physical,' she said, 'but all the while her brain's working. She's not deliberately thinking, it's her unconscious mind, rerunning everything that's happened, going round and round. By the end of the day she's mentally drained, and her body feels it too.'

That made sense, anyway. I didn't mind those sessions with her. It did help to talk to someone outside.

Another time, I remember being in my nan's flat, above the shop. I was sat in her old rocking chair, going backwards and forwards, backwards and forwards, staring the wall, and humming to myself. I found it soothing. And I needed soothing. When I wasn't zonked out like a zombie I was in a screaming fit, taking it out on Mum and Dad. Rage just bubbling up, spitting out through my mouth. One day I actually got on the phone to my social worker, yelling, 'Get me out of here, I hate these people, they're not my mum and dad.'

God, what a pain I was. But Mum and Dad stuck it out, for months on end. By Christmas, I was thinking I must be better, the worst of it was over. We had a nice time, and Stevie was back home too. I know Mum and Dad had told him about what happened to me, and he'd freaked. To my face, Stevie was his old self, joshing around, though maybe a bit quieter than usual. It's not in his nature to say anything emotional, at least not out loud.

Maybe it was the new year that made me, and Mum and Dad too, think about making a change in our lives.

We were talking, and I just said, 'We could get away, leave this place.'

'Yeah,' said Dad straight away. 'Leave memories behind, start a new life. Put everything behind us. Even leave the country – we'd be well away.'

'That's a bit drastic,' said Mum, but she could see the point to it. If I was away from where everything bad had happened, I wouldn't keep getting reminded. The memories would fade.

After a lot of talk, we fixed on Greece, Corfu. Mum and Dad had good friends who lived there, and they helped arrange the purchase of an apartment for us. Dad sold up the shop, and got a good price. 'You can be ladies of leisure,' he joked to me and Mum.

In June, just a month after my fifteenth birthday, we were all set. We didn't sell our house – we wouldn't burn all our boats, just in case. Nan would be living there, as her flat had gone with the shop, and Auntie Sue would join her. We were all looking forward to the move, we were sure this was the best thing to do.

What we couldn't know was that it would be just like sweeping stuff under the carpet. We weren't just travelling to a new place, we were running away from the old one, and trouble was coming with us.

The trouble was in my head, my screwed-up mind – and I couldn't exactly leave my head behind! Not that it showed up at first. Things seemed okay for a while. The weather was lovely and warm, which helped. I've always liked the sun. Then there was all the novelty of settling in, finding our way around. We knew we weren't on holiday, though. I didn't want to just laze around all the time, and joined a local college, a private one where they spoke English. At home I wouldn't have been allowed to leave school before I was sixteen – not that I'd been going anyway after the Ahmed business. Here in Greece, things seemed more relaxed, and I joined a hair and beauty course. Maybe I'd forget A levels and be a beautician. Women always want to look good. I do.

Meanwhile, Mum and Dad had landed part-time jobs, helping to look after holiday lets, mostly big villas, all very posh. They loved it, and everything seemed to be going along fine.

Then, I couldn't put my finger on exactly when, maybe six months after we arrived, I started to feel funny – strange, I mean. I found I couldn't eat properly. Every time I tried, my throat closed up and I thought I'd be sick. The weight dropped off me, till one morning, in the bright sunlight, as I sat at the breakfast table in a sleeveless top, Mum looked at me and said, 'Good God, Emma! What's happening to you! You're nowt but skin and bone!'

That was true. And I was tired again, tired out. I kept getting flashbacks of what had happened in town, in the mall, in the park...and each time I was flooded with the feelings I thought I'd got rid of. I was that unhappy, I could have just ended it all, to make the pain and the misery go away.

'I want to go home,' I moaned to Mum and Dad. I didn't care that I'd thought it was a good idea to come out here. I didn't care I'd be upsetting the apple cart again. On top of everything else, I was homesick, I wanted my home. My real home, I mean, where I felt safe. Mum felt homesick too, by this time. She was missing home and family. Dad was having a high old time, himself, in his element with all the ex-pats out here, but when he picked up on what me and Mum were feeling, there was no question. Like he always did, he put us first.

'We'll go home then,' he said. 'If you're sure, Emma? You'll face it again?'

'Yeah.'

'Right, then. I'll start on paperwork.'

It was while we were waiting for the sale to go through that I hit another kind of rock bottom. It was evening, and we were sitting in our living room, three floors up. The sliding doors were open to the balcony outside, which was very pretty, all fancy wrought iron, painted green. There was a nice breeze blowing in. All of a sudden, I don't know where it came from, I was on my feet, screaming.

'If I don't go home now I'll jump off balcony! I will!'

I headed for the doors and Mum and Dad jumped up and held me back. All I can say is that there and then I meant it, everything was too much, I couldn't bear any more.

They took me to a doctor, of course, but he was no good. I couldn't make him understand what was wrong with me. If I knew myself. He probably thought I was just some hysterical young Brit with a touch of the sun.

'It'll be better at home, love,' Mum kept telling me. And I had to believe her.

I was terrified, but it was like something was clearing in my head. Bits and pieces came back to me, things the psychologist had said. At the time I'd just nodded, said, 'Yeah,' didn't think deeply about it. But when we got back home, there was a turning point. I got sent to a clinic in town for young people with behavioural difficulties and eating disorders, and the doctors and therapists were brilliant.

It took quite a while, but bit by bit, over months and months, with their help, I managed to work through it.

It was a mistake to pretend it hadn't happened. All that sweeping under the carpet might give you a quick fix, but it doesn't mend you. And running away doesn't work either. You just take the problem with you. New surroundings might help for a while, be a distraction, but your past will catch you up. That's what happened to me.

When I had to talk about it before, it was like I was talking about somebody else, another young girl. I had to set up a wall to protect myself, put a distance between me and those men, close myself down, so to speak. Now I had to face it, accept it happened, till I could say, out loud, 'I was a prostitute, a child prostitute. Men had sex with me for money.' But, and this is really important, 'It wasn't my fault. They exploited me, tricked me, frightened me and hurt me. I was the innocent one.' I had to deal with the fact that I'd been betrayed, had my friendship and trust flung back in my face. The rapes, the physical part, were bad enough, but in a way it was the betrayal that hurt the most, and was hardest to deal with.

Once all this had really sunk in, there was another step. This happened to me, but it doesn't define me as a person. I was me, Emma, before it happened, and I'm still Emma, I'm my own person. Of course my life took a different turn, and I'll never know how it would have gone if I hadn't got mixed up with criminals. But I can't change the past. All I can do is look ahead, plan for the future, make the best of it.

As I told my mum and dad, 'They might have stolen my teenage years, but the rest of my life belongs to me.'

EPILOGUE
My New World

So I got my life back. I can't pretend it's been easy, but I've had a lot of help, and have always been able to rely on the love and support of my family. Writing this book, having to think about everything all over again, has helped me sort things out in my head. More than anything, I've tried to set out just how a good girl from a loving home could be drawn into this other world, an underworld of crime. If you read the papers, you'd think that the only girls who get hooked are those in care, or from dysfunctional families. If my book does nothing else, I want it said loud and clear: what happened to me could happen to anyone. Your child, your sister, your friend – even you yourself, if you're young and naive enough, like me.

What happened to me wasn't an isolated case of a paedophile taking advantage of a child. That's really terrible, of course. The man's sick in his head, a child suffers at his hands, and that's wrong in every way.

The difference with me was that I was caught up in organised crime. A paedophile grooms his victim, we know that much, but I was groomed by a slow process that involved lots of different people. It was so gradual, I was never aware of it. I mean, if a thirty-year-old guy had come up to me, out of the blue, at the mall, I'd have run a mile. No, I got used to the nice young lads first off, looked forward to their company. They seemed friendly, harmless. And I'm sure most of them were. The last thing I want to do is make out that all the Asian lads I met were up to no good, all part of a plan. I can't say it too strongly. My abusers happened to be Muslims, because in this part of the world there was a large population of Muslims, and in every community you get bad sorts.

Among those Asian lads there were enough of them willing to play a part. Introduce me gradually to a wider circle. Every guy I met was linked in some way to another, so I never met an out-and-out stranger. That lulls you into a sense of security. And it shows that what happened to me was planned very carefully. No rushing, just gradually getting me to a stage where I was trapped. They played on me wanting to be grown up, like a lot of kids do. The drink and the dope were just part of what I thought was glamorous, like you see in glossy magazines and on TV. All the time I was getting deeper and deeper in, like an animal stalked by a pack of lions, getting cut off from anything and anyone who might have helped me. And what was in it for them? Money, of course, it all comes down to money. And sex on tap. I reckon some of those guys high up the chain were raking in thousands, and had the pick of the girls.

I've already talked about the 'if's in my life. They're important, so I'll go over them again.

First off, it was my choice of friends. Joanne was the link to this other world. I don't like to think she knew all about it. I hope she was just trying to get in with the lads, as they never fancied her for herself, and that hurt her. Maybe she closed her eyes a lot, as she did seem to want to be my friend. On the other hand, the hard view is that she knew all about it, and coldly carried out instructions to bring along a little blue-eyed blonde. Whatever the truth, if I hadn't hung out with Joanne, I would never have had that first toe in the water.

Then my family set-up was perfect to make me more vulnerable. Don't think for a minute I'm blaming my mum and dad for working so hard. Of course not, even if they blame themselves, to this day. It was just that as they were out most of the day, it was easy for me to tell lies, to pull the wool over their eyes. If they'd had regular nine-to-five jobs, they would have known I was away out a lot of the time. No wonder the bad guys wanted to know all about my family. Even Stevie leaving home to work, that was useful. If he'd been around, he would have picked up on stuff.

Then there's me, of course. I was just the right age, they knew that. If I'd been younger, I wouldn't have been allowed the freedom I had, and I probably would have been too shy to talk to boys in public anyway. If I'd been older, I would have had more sense, more experience, wouldn't have fallen for it all, wouldn't have believed the lies they told about my parents not loving me. As it was, there was me, a cocky, know-it-all young teenager wanting the grown-up life without any of the skills to handle it.

Perfect set-up. And these bad guys are expert – they've had a lot of practice. Where Tarik and his mates were concerned, I must have just been the latest girl on the conveyor belt.

As I said, it was when I was in hospital the first time that I realised other girls had got into trouble like me, or even worse. I might have thought I was alone, but I was just one of many. I learned a lot more later on, when my mum happened to read an article by a woman whose daughter had been trapped into the sex trade. The poor girl was murdered, at just seventeen, in the early 1990s. Her mother, Irene Ivison, set up an organisation called CROP, the Coalition for the Removal of Pimping. Mum saw the connection with what had happened to me, and got in touch with them. A member called Jane came to visit me. She was a real friend, a lifeline. She understood better than most what I'd been through. She asked me to go to meetings at CROP, to talk to other people and hear their stories, and I was very happy to do that.

Some of the stories I heard, though, shocked me – such cruelty and trickery. There was one girl I heard of who reminded me of the one my gynaecologist had talked about, the one who had the bleach poured inside her. This other girl had had lighter fuel poured over her face, and set alight. Think of it.

Then there were the parents. It was heartbreaking to hear them. 'How do we get her back?' they'd ask me, their eyes pleading. All I could do was tell my story, how I got out, say I was like an alcoholic or a heroin addict.

'I'm not stronger than anyone else, don't think that. It's just that I hit my rock bottom, and I couldn't fall any more. I had to come up again, or die, and bad though I felt, I really did want to go on living. Maybe it'll be the same for your daughter, but everyone's got a different breaking point.'

A lot of these girls are trapped by the way they feel about their pimps. At first, he would've seemed like a regular boyfriend, paying attention, being charming, till the girl's fallen for him, she's in love, she thinks. For all the man puts her through, she kids herself he still loves her, and she doesn't want to lose him. It's like another kind of drug, I suppose. Well, there I was lucky. My age might have made me vulnerable in one way – not being streetwise – but at least I was too young for the falling-in-love bit, I wasn't caught up in sexual attraction. When I knew Tarik for what he was, and then Ahmed, I hated them. It was easier for me to want to get out of their clutches.

I realised all over again how lucky I was to escape. Most girls don't. They're trapped in much the same way as I was, and then forced to have sex with man after man after man, even hundreds of them, till they're used up. They go from the stage I was at – being handed over to individual men by my pimp – to working in flats. Then they're on the streets, and in the gutter, hopeless addicts. They either die from disease, or they're killed by their pimps – though even women too damaged for sex have their uses. I heard of them having to swallow condoms full of cocaine, then visiting someone in prison, shitting out the condom in the prison toilet and washing it in the sink, before handing it over. I'd never imagined anything like it.

Or, of course, girls disappear. Well, I say disappear, but here in Britain, in the twenty-first century, it's not easy to actually disappear. There's all that CCTV, and a body can be hard to hide. The more I heard, the more I thought those girls must have been smuggled out of the country. You hear of sex trafficking, bringing girls into the country, so it must work the other way. Wherever there's a paying customer, there's a pimp. But there hasn't been that much publicity about girls being moved round Britain.

The BBC made a *Panorama* programme about this side of the sex trade in 2008, how girls as young as twelve are being groomed for the sex trade on the streets of Britain. I was asked to take part, through CROP, and I jumped at the chance of telling people about what can happen in this day and age. The more people know about it, the better. I was disguised in the interviews, and an actress spoke my words. I'm still very wary of making my identity public. It's not just the criminals I might have pissed off in the past, it's the risk of attracting other people, for all the wrong reasons, of having fingers pointed at me.

The whole experience of abuse has left its mark, of course, and I'm much more cautious these days. More like an old granny than a carefree twenty-something! Always keeping a careful eye on places and people, till I'm sure I'm safe. But I can live with that. After everything, I've a lot going for me. Life is good – in a way I never could have imagined when I was trapped. For now, I'm still living with my mum and dad, but in a lovely new house, miles away from where I grew up. Nan and Auntie Sue are still nearby, and we're all close again. I've learned to drive and that gives me more independence. I've got lots of friends I hang out with, and a boyfriend. Of course, I'd worried that I wouldn't be able to have a normal relationship when I met someone I cared for, that the abuse I'd suffered would have screwed me up too much. But things have been working out well, touch wood. Maybe it was the therapy I had, maybe the fact that I was so young I could be resilient. Whatever, he's a great guy, and (though I don't want to sound like one of those people who say 'Some of my best friends are...') happens to be Asian. I'll say it again, it was never about race or nationality. A man's a criminal and that's that.

In fact that's what CROP makes a big point of. Criminals, traffickers, pimps, they come from all sorts of ethnic backgrounds and cultures, just like the paying punters who keep up the demand. And demand and supply seem never-ending, feeding off each other. Organisations like CROP work full out, fighting against sexual exploitation – and it's a huge, uphill fight.

Like lots of other people who campaign against sex abuse, it does my head in that not enough seems to be done. You only have to look at the figures for rape convictions to get the idea that sex abuse isn't taken seriously enough in this country. I think it's as low as 6 per cent once a case finally gets to court. Lots of rapes don't even get that far, of course. There seem to be so many obstacles in the way.

I know it's not enough to sit around talking about it. When people hear about my story and say to me, 'Oh, it's awful, how terrible, how you must have suffered,' I feel like saying, 'I don't want your pity. I've survived, I'm fine now and I'm gonna have a good life. What we need is action, and fast.'

Not that I know what action, exactly. I'm not a politician, but there must be something the government, the police and social services can do to root out these criminal gangs. Set up dedicated squads, go undercover...and, first of all, take it seriously. Respect the girls and women. Those gangs are like a virus in our society, bringing nothing but heartache after heartache for so many people, so many families. And it's not just the sex trade, of course. Where there's prostitution, there's drugs, and guns. Young girls raped, young boys shot in the street – they're all linked, they're all part of the same rotten underworld.

While writing this book, I've grown more and more convinced that what I want to do is somehow help girls who weren't as lucky as me – and I do mean lucky. Maybe get proper qualifications and work in social services or the law. I want to go home in the evening thinking, 'That's made a difference. That'll give her a chance.' I'll be doing what I can to get what I want for me, for you, for all of us.

A better world.

Afterword

It's been ten years now since I first met Tarik, and two since this book was first published. When I was going through the bad times, I couldn't have imagined I'd get to the end of them, let alone build up a whole new life and a professional career. But I'm pleased to say I'm now doing the kind of work where I can use what happened to me to help other people, and it doesn't get better than that. In fact I'll go so far as to say that what could have destroyed me has, in a way, been the making of me.

I'd worked with CROP and other organisations on a voluntary basis before my book was published, but afterwards things really took off. I've used my experience to advise professionals – social workers, police, politicians, charity workers, teachers – on what to look out for in child abuse cases, how best to deal with the issues. I've taken part in seminars and made speeches at conferences. And I've talked directly to other victims, and potential victims. I've even advised on a storyline for *EastEnders*!

The first edition of this book was called *The End of My World*, as it did seem when I was going through the worst that my world had finished. It hadn't, of course. I'm hoping this new edition will reach even more people, and I decided to call it *Exploited* – because, let's face it, that's what actually went on, and it's still going on for young girls today.

This year a court case hit the headlines and got the general public talking, bringing the whole issue of child sexual exploitation out into the open. The *Times* newspaper broke the story, and did us all a great service.

It was the Rochdale case, where a gang of men in the town had been preying on underage girls, grooming them and trafficking them for sexual abuse. As I read the details in the paper, it was so horribly familiar. Target the girl, ply her with drink and drugs, give her gifts and money, lure her to flats and give her to men for sex...The victims were picked up at takeaway shops rather than a shopping centre, and most if not all of the girls had deprived and dysfunctional backgrounds – otherwise, it could have been my story. Another difference was that most of the accused men were actually convicted, and sent to jail. Result!

As the details emerged, along with the shock and outrage came all the questions: How long has this been going on? Did the police know about it? Was there a cover-up? What else don't we know? Good questions. And then the elephant in the room: the race card, as nearly all the men were of Pakistani origin, and all the victims were white.

As I've said before, this is not about race but about crime, and bad men. But it's a sensitive issue, and I'm sure the fear of seeming racist stopped some people from speaking out when they should have. Political correct-ness and all that. I'm very glad people are now speaking openly about it, having an intelligent debate.

When I read that one of the Rochdale victims had gone to the police earlier, but the CPS had refused to prosecute, that struck a chord. In the first case we brought against my abusers, we dropped the charges because of intimidation. In the second, the CPS thought there wasn't enough evidence to convict. We certainly thought at the time that the right people weren't exactly busting a gut to protect us, to get at the truth of the matter.

Then there's the whole question of what the public does or doesn't know about child sexual abuse – and what it doesn't want to know. Don't get me wrong, I realise that nobody wants to think about something so nasty. If you're not a professional in the field, or you're not affected personally, then why would you? After all, what did me and my family do when the second case collapsed? Run away to Corfu, hoping to put all the bad things behind us, but really taking them with us. Sweeping everything under the carpet as it was just so awful. But bad things don't go away just because you shut your eyes, whether it's happening to you or somebody else. I read in the paper that a politician, Tim Loughton, the Minister for Children and Families, used those exact words – 'sweeping under the carpet'. No more of that, he said, and I hope it's true.

After my book was published, and again following the publicity about the Rochdale case, a lot of the feedback was all about surprise as well as shock – 'I didn't know this sort of thing went on.' 'This must be something new.' People then go on to say: 'This is awful, but it could never happen to my daughter.' Or my niece, or anyone I care about. And I'd want to say to them, 'Why not? How does being a relative of yours protect a girl from abuse? Look at me, the classic good girl from a loving home.' I'd tell my concerned parents that I'd be at a friend's house, while really I'd be in a car with a couple of men, smoking joints and drinking vodka and thinking I was having a good time. So you think your kid is staying at a friend's house? How do you know he or she isn't one of the gang in the bus shelter knocking back cheap cider? God knows, there's enough of them around every night.

Of course, if a girl doesn't have a stable family background, if she's deprived of love and proper attention, then she will be more vulnerable, more needy. But what people – I mean parents most of all – have to recognise is that their precious child is not immune to bad influences. They might like to think that there must have been something wrong in the way I was brought up, my parents didn't look after me properly, and they would never make that mistake. But I say: 'Don't kid yourself!'

Teenagers break the rules, that's what they do. They go places they shouldn't go, they do things they shouldn't do. They drink, they smoke, they experiment with drugs and sex. There may be kids out there who are squeaky clean and never lie, but to my knowledge I've never met any.

I've started saying, 'Teenagers today...' like some old fart, and I'm only twenty-three. But I swear things have got more pressurised for kids since my day, especially with the internet. How many parents today are properly clued up about the technology? There's always a lot of stuff in the papers about online porn, and how children should be protected, but do parents really know how their children use the social networking sites like Facebook and Twitter?

There are thirteen-year-olds putting photos of themselves on Facebook, wearing bikinis or their underwear, posing like they're models. They count up the comments, how many people like them. They want to be popular, and sexy gets them popular, they think. But they're too young to know what they're really doing, which is making themselves vulnerable. They might as well advertise themselves as available. I know a lot of girls who go in for this, they talk to me. And I remember when I was thirteen, I just knew that I knew it all. So it's up to adults to monitor what they do, to make sure they're not putting themselves in danger.

I really will sound like an old fart now, but I don't care. It's about time we all drew the line, made it clear that it's not all right for such young girls to think they have to be sexy. They're children. And as for actually having sex – I reckon that most sixteen-year-olds aren't ready for it, let alone younger kids. It's a big part of life, it's important, the most intimate you can be. But too many of the children I meet seem to devalue it, treat it as something mechanical, just another thing to do, like buying ice cream, with no emotional involvement and no after effects. In schools I've heard children as young as twelve talk about friends with benefits! For those who don't know, it's having sex with someone just because you feel like it – no relationship, not even friendship. Doesn't get more casual than that. Then they mention in passing sexual acts like blowjobs and teabagging (look it up if you have to).

Even allowing for teenage bravado it's an attitude that shocks me to the core. Whether they're actually getting up to it or not, it's an attitude that cheapens sex and normalises abuse.

What really makes me angry is the way many adults approach the whole issue. They seem to think that as long as the boy wears a condom, nobody catches a disease and the girl doesn't get pregnant, anything goes. I remember there was a national campaign a while back to lower the rate of teenage pregnancy, and the message to girls was: 'If he respects you, he'll put a condom on.' I thought no, don't let's look just at lowering teenage pregnancy, let's look at what issues are behind so many kids having sex. Why look at the easy solutions when the real issue is that these kids shouldn't be having sex at all?

I know that if I was thirteen, and saw an advert like that, I'd think that the message was: It's all right to have sex, as long as you're careful. Have sex with anyone, as long as he puts on a johnny. But as an adult woman I know the real meaning of respect: nobody should be forced into having sex before they're ready. Made to think they're abnormal if they don't. It seems to me that all that gets talked about is pregnancy and STIs and contraception. Well, let's talk to them about how it might affect them mentally. Emotionally.

What would a thirteen-year-old girl say about her first sexual experience if she was being truthful? I reckon for most girls it wouldn't be about the pleasure, it'd be more like, 'Well, I've been going out with this boy at school who's in the year above me, and he really wanted sex and he said he'd use a condom, so that's all right. And all my friends have done it thousands of times and I don't want to be left out, so I said okay. And I lost my virginity in a field, up against a tree, and it lasted about sixty seconds and he's spotty and horrible and if that's what sex is like, I never want to do it again. Ever.'

So she won't catch chlamydia and she won't get pregnant, but how does she feel? Used? Dirty? The average age for first sex these days is apparently thirteen or fourteen. The longer this is accepted in society, the more normal it'll seem. Quite apart from the effect on vulnerable children, it also makes it easier for abusers to get their way. A girl forced to have sex might think, 'I hate this but he's telling me it's normal, everyone does it, so stop crying and just get on with it.' He's telling her that, and so is society.

I do realise I'm making big generalisations here – there are lots of adults who don't go along with this attitude, and there must be children who do resist all the peer pressure. But look around. Messages pouring out on TV, films, magazines, billboards and of course online: sex sells. It's adults telling children that, and it's not healthy.

Do I have a solution? I wish. Just how this flood of images and propaganda can be stopped, or even slowed down, I don't know. But I can keep speaking out, be one of the voices calling for change, in my own small way stand up and be counted.

Everything I say comes from what I experienced, and what I've observed. I don't have paper qualifications, but I can look any professional in the eye and give my opinion. And I'll give it straight. I don't care if you're the prime minister of England, if I don't agree with you, I'll tell you. I'm not looking over my shoulder in case I don't toe some party line and offend someone. In fact, I think we spend too much time these days trying not to offend people. Political correctness once got in the way of justice for the Rochdale victims, and it's the victims I'm concerned about.

Sometimes I think the only people who can be offended are the victims themselves. Take the expression 'child prostitute' for a start. There's no such thing! No child wakes up in the morning and says to herself, 'I'm a bit bored, I'll go out and get a pimp and I'll have sex with strange men and give my pimp all the money they pay me.' Sex with children is abuse, and a crime, committed not by the child but the man who rapes her.

And in law, abusers have rights, human rights. In my experience, they're not always extended to the victim.

I once showed a video of one of my police interviews to a friend of mine. I'd asked my solicitor for copies of all the evidence the police held, including their interviews with me and with my abusers. In this particular video, the police were questioning me about what happened to me, and weren't being what you'd call very sympathetic. This friend used to be a member of a gang, and had done some bad things, armed robbery and drugs, but he'd decided to turn his life round and was going straight. As he watched the video, he was shaking his head and sort of laughing.

'I'm not really laughing,' he said to me. 'I'm just gobsmacked at the way they're talking to you. I was treated with more respect than you were – and I'm the robber and you're the victim. And you're just a child!'

Where sex is involved in a crime, the questioning is as much about establishing the victim's innocence as it is the abuser's guilt. Honest, she was asking for it, look at the way she was dressed, and she told me she was seventeen…I know this happened to me ten years ago, and people working with children at risk have got more aware, more sensitive, since then but old attitudes haven't gone away.

The way I see it, this can show up when a young girl known to be at risk is being questioned by the police or a social worker. She might suddenly switch from saying she was targeted by young men, and instead say that her dad's been abusing her. She could well be making this up to get the heat off the real perpetrator, who might have told her to say this. But then all hell breaks loose, everyone piles in and the dad is removed from the home. Everyone is taking the girl seriously now. But when she'd said that a whole lot of men had been having sex with her, there wasn't any rush to investigate. What's that about?

It's as if the prospect of having sex with her dad is so awful, so disgusting, she couldn't possibly want it, so she's automatically a victim. But when it comes to having sex with one strange man after another, who knows? Maybe it's her choice. So in the first case the focus is all on the dad, what kind of man is he? But in the second case, the focus is all on the girl, what kind of girl is she? Is she a tart? Does she put it about a bit? It's like I said before – no child can be a tart, no child can be a prostitute. She's a victim of adult abusers.

It's taken years of talking to people of all backgrounds, and listening to their stories, to get to my way of thinking, to what I believe. When I was first recovering, in my teens, I was quite happy to help out at CROP and other set-ups, just telling my story and trying to think of advice I could give. I suppose it was a kind of therapy for me too. I was on medication at the time, unable to work and living on benefits. As I grew up, I thought more and more deeply about everything, but still it never occurred to me that I could turn my experience into a way of earning my living. I was happy that I had the chance to write my book, get my story out there and be part of the debate.

But then the woman in charge of training at a local council project I'd been involved in asked me to do what's called life story work. This was basically telling my story to social workers, trainees and qualified people, and answering their questions, to help them improve their skills. I had a proper contract, for ten hours a week, and the going rate for the job. I was really chuffed. It gave me the confidence to think that what I was doing was valued by other people.

After a few months, word must have got around, and I started working for other people, again getting paid. One long-term contract was with a local police force, a training programme to increase awareness of child sex abuse. I helped train all the officers, from the lowest to the highest, giving a PowerPoint presentation followed by a question-and-answer session. With my experience in mind, I made a point of telling them to watch out for young girls in a car with grown men. If the girl is obviously around thirteen or fourteen, and there are four adult men in the car, and it's late at night, then that could ring alarm bells. What's going on there? And if it's four Asian or black men and one white girl – or of course four white men and one Asian or black girl – there's less likely to be a family connection. There could be a perfectly innocent explanation, but if the officer thinks there's anything remotely suspicious, then go with that instinct.

Another thing I told them was that if they come across a car parked in an isolated area, and again there's a young girl with even one grown man, don't just ask the girl through the window, 'Is everything all right?' She'll only say, 'Yeah, fine, he's my boyfriend.' Ask them to step out of the car and have a word with them separately. She's more likely to say that she's worried if he can't hear her.

I know it's tricky. An honest man shouldn't be made to feel like a criminal, but a child's safety could be at stake – and the officer doesn't have to go in all guns blazing. Is the only alternative to look the other way and hope for the best? Surely it's better to tread on a few toes and rescue a child from abuse?

From life story work and training sessions, I went on

to speak at various seminars and conferences in front of hundreds of people. I must admit I was nervous to start with, but then I realised no, I've got to get up and say my piece, speak not only for me but all the other victims, to get our point across. When those people high up in their organisations are drafting their policies, writing their procedures, it's really important that they hear this. In October 2010 I spoke at a conference given by a project that supports women and children who've suffered sexual abuse. The theme was 'Hearing and Listening: Enabling young people's voice and influence in sexual exploitation services', which for me sums up the need. I got very positive feedback from that, people really seemed to appreciate what I said, and that was a boost to my confidence. So when the next one was in Rome, a month or so later, I didn't feel so worried. This was for the Council of Europe campaign to stop sexual violence against children. It was an eye-opener – just how wide-spread this abuse is. It seems to be a worldwide issue.

Since then, I've had pretty regular work, enough to support myself and come off benefits. That was a real turning point, made me feel independent. I suppose I'm a kind of freelance consultant, as I'm involved in a wide network of organisations and services. I never know who's going to call on me next.

Sometimes people ask me if I ever get tired of

working in what is, let's face it, a very depressing field, especially as I'm still so young. Things can get heavy. Then I moan to my mum and dad, 'Wish I worked in a chuffing sandwich factory!' But that doesn't last long – my passion for the campaign keeps me going.

Mind you, I could do without some aspects of the job. So many meetings...I've been sat in meetings where the talk goes round in circles and you could warm the town hall with all the hot air. My dad agrees with me there. He's still got a full-time job, but he takes time out to sit on advisory boards and committees dealing with child abuse issues. Like me, and like my mum too, he's been galvanised by what happened; he wants to use it to help make the family's voice heard as well as the victim's. It's not always that easy. 'Talk, talk, talk,' he comes back saying, 'and that bloody jargon they use...'

I know what he means. People using jargon so they sound clever, as if they know what they're talking about. I've sat in on meetings where parents and children involved in a case are invited by social services to make their voice heard. Nine times out of ten they just sit there, not knowing what's going on and scared of looking stupid if they do say something. And it's their lives being discussed. But of course, a lot of good work is being done. It's just that I get impatient with policy papers and resolutions and all that kind of thing. I'm itching to get things done, to see a change on the front line and not in a meeting room!

Something that was a lot more fun than meetings happened last year, the time I was asked to advise on the *EastEnders* storyline, when Whitney was being exploited by her boyfriend Rob. Me and a couple of other girls who'd been abused were invited to London to talk to the writers and meet the actors. I'm a huge *EastEnders* fan, and I was thrilled that it was prepared to tackle such a difficult issue. I must say all the TV people were very committed to the story, very sensitive to it, and wanted to get it right. The writers had read my book and they had lots of questions for us. I reckon they did a really good job. The way Rob took advantage of Whitney, then gained her trust and lured her on so he could sell her to his 'mates' was powerful, very realistic. Whitney was the right mix of vulnerable and trusting, and totally convincing when her dreams were shattered. Rob was perfect as the guy who on the surface is charming and charismatic, with just a hint of something dark lurking in him. There was a mini-episode catch-up to the story for Comic Relief, which funds charities fighting abuse, and that made a huge impact. As a bonus, us three girls were invited to the Comic Relief show – our brush with the stars!

I realised later what an impression the storyline had made when I was talking to some girls about abuse, and they said, 'That happened to Whitney!' It was a good way in, a good way of bringing it home to young people.

I talk to a lot of girls' groups. I find the best way to get through to them, to break the hold the boyfriend has on them, is to identify with them. 'I'm a girl,' I say, 'a bit older than you but still a girl. I know what it's like to fancy a boy, to want a good time.' I tell them my story and then say something like this:

'If a boy really likes you, and he wants you to be his girlfriend, then what he'll do is ask you out on a date. Maybe see a film, or have a meal out, or go bowling. He'll be proud to be seen with you, he'll hold your hand. What he won't do is hide you away in a flat and invite all his mates to come round and have sex with you, or ask you to give all his mates a blowjob in the car. That's not normal. A real boyfriend will care for you, respect you. He won't push you into having sex. If he really likes you, and puts you first, and your relationship goes that far, then you'll have sex when you're both ready. He definitely, *definitely*, will not get his friends to have sex with you, or even think about it. He'll want you to himself because you're so important to him.'

It usually clicks with the girls, and they realise they're being used. At the same time I try to encourage them, build up their confidence, tell them they deserve so much better – they're young and beautiful with their whole life ahead of them.

You might be thinking that something's missing from all this talk. Boys. What about them?

I've spoken to boys as a youth worker, doing prevention work. One time I remember especially was a group of fifteen- and sixteen-year-olds in Manchester. They were suspected of grooming girls for older men, enticing them in, so I told them my story and laid it on the line.

'You think this is fun, you get to have sex with girls and money to buy your flash gear. Great. But the girl is underage, and what happens when she reports to the police that she's been raped? The police come round to arrest you for abusing a child, and you go on the sex offenders' register. Not so much fun now, is it?'

Their balls hit the floor. They realised for the first time just what they were getting involved in. They were all Asian, so I did wonder what their response would be to my experience, whether they'd respect me. Turned out they did, and they thanked me and asked lots of questions.

They all said they were surprised that I'd turned out

like I had. I get this a lot – people seem to think I shouldn't have become a decent person living a good life. I should be running around swigging vodka and breeding child after child with different men while living on benefits. If I want to get one message through to victims of abuse, it's that the experience doesn't have to define them. They can go on to lead a good life, find love, have their own family and create a stable home.

Talking of which…I've had some wonderful news: I'm pregnant! Me and my boyfriend are over the moon, and so are our families. We've got great plans. And it set me thinking – bearing in mind what happened to me, what would I tell my new baby about relationships?

If I have a boy, he'll definitely be taught to respect women, just as his dad respects his mum. He'll know that women are equal to men. When he meets a girl he really likes, then he should treat her well, just as he'd like someone to treat his sister or his mum. That girl could be someone's sister and in time she'll be someone's mum.

If I have a girl, I'll tell her to always stand up for herself, always respect men but never feel that they're better than her, or that they can control her. When she meets a boy she likes, her first real boyfriend, she shouldn't rush in there. Just enjoy life, don't try growing up too fast, enjoy being young – it doesn't last for long. Have fun with boys but don't take things too far, don't be too serious, the right one will come in time. Being sexy isn't the be-all and end-all.

The baby's due early next year. Meanwhile, I'm happy working on what comes my way. Most recently I was asked to give a quote for a government progress report about tackling child sexual exploitation – part of the fall-out from the Rochdale case. I gave it a lot of thought, trying to be fair, and I came up with this:

'At long last I'm happy to say I feel that child sexual exploitation is finally being recognised by agencies and professionals across the country. We are beginning to tackle this issue but we are not all the way there yet, and now is the time for action. This is never an easy subject, but let's not run scared, let's start as we mean to go on and make some changes.'

And I want to add, 'Hurry up!' Those changes mustn't take too long. It's my greatest hope that my baby grows up in a better, safer, world.

Emma Jackson,
2012

AUTHOR'S NOTE

What happened to me is in the past, but the problem of abuse and sexual exploitation of girls and young women is still going on – and it's getting worse. The girls are getting even younger. If you yourself are in the same situation as I was, or if you're worried that someone you know might be, then there are organisations that are ready to help.

First there's CROP, which has been a huge help to me. It works alongside parents, carers and the wider family of child exploitation victims. It's based in Leeds, but it's a good first point of call for anyone in the country.

CROP
34 York Road
Leeds LS9 8TA
Tel: 0113 240 3040
Web: www.cropuk.org.uk
Email: info@cropuk.org.uk

Next there's the national charity, Barnado's, which offers a whole range of help for children in trouble.

Barnardo's
Tanners Lane
Barkingside
Ilford
Essex 1G6 1QG
Tel: 020 8550 8822
Web: www.barnados.org.uk

Then there's an organisation that offers general help for anybody affected by crime, directly or indirectly.

Victim Support National Centre
Hallam House
56–60 Hallam Street
London W1W 6JL
Tel: 020 7268 0200
Supportline: 0845 30 30 900
Web: www.victimsupport.org.uk

Any of these organisations will offer you advice and practical help. So make that call. If it's for somebody else, even if it's just a doubt in your mind, still make that call. You could be saving a child from feeling like it's the end of their world.